LOYALTY UNPLUGGED

LOYALTY UNPLUGGED

How to Get, Keep & Grow All Four Generations

Adwoa K. Buahene and Giselle Kovary

n-gen People Performance Inc.

To order additional copies of this book, contact:
Xlibris Corporation
1-888-795-4274
www.Xlibris.com
Orders@Xlibris.com
35499

Dedication

Collectively, n-gen People Performance Inc. has many people
to thank for their support. From peers to friends to clients,
there have been many champions of our business,
our approach, and us. We thank you.

We dedicate this book to our parents who, though Traditionalists,
believe in our entrepreneurial spirit and support us one hundred percent.

For you,

Germaine and Andy Kovary

Ingrid and Kwame Buahene

CONTENTS

Section I: Setting the Stage

Section II: How to Get 'Em

Section III: How to Keep 'Em

Section IV: How to Grow 'Em

Introduction

Loyalty is dead. Loyalty is unplugged. In music, *unplugged* means returning from synthetic (electronic) sound back to the acoustic (raw) sound. For us, *unplugging loyalty* means exposing, talking about, and evaluating loyalty in a new, raw, and pragmatic way. We believe employees are still loyal, but where they place their loyalty has shifted. This shift impacts an organization's productivity and performance. Leaders should be less concerned with creating a loyal workforce but more focused on creating an engaged workforce that can respond effectively and efficiently to market drivers. In our knowledge economy, organizations that create the best people strategies will find themselves ahead of their competition. Getting, keeping, and growing the right people for the right job at the right time is arguably the key to maintaining and gaining competitive advantage.

To successfully design and execute people strategies that work, there are two key considerations that need to be layered onto all analysis, design, development and implementation. First consider the fact that your employee workforce is segmented into four distinct generational cohorts. The cohorts are as follows:

Traditionalists: 1922-1945
Baby Boomers: 1946-1964
Gen Xers: 1965-1980
Gen Ys: 1981-2000

Each cohort has different values, characteristics, and expectations that shape its generational identity. The identity defines a cohort's value and belief system of life, love, and work. For your organization to truly engage your people, you need to understand how each cohort behaves and responds to you as an employer. Conceptually, we have simply borrowed an approach used by marketing departments. Marketers segment their customer groups (i.e., geography, age, and ethnicity) and design marketing strategies and messages that target each segment. We have taken the principle of segmentation and have applied it internally to your workforce. Simply put, you have four employee markets whose values, expectations, and behaviors impact your people practices.

Second, you must understand what you can do to tap into each cohort in order to drive engagement. For this reason, we have incorporated the concept of organizational engagement. While others focus on what engaged employees do to demonstrate commitment and loyalty to an organization, we argue that you won't have engaged employees until your organization demonstrates engagement (transparency, responsiveness, and partnering). This book explores how to demonstrate the characteristics of organizational engagement in getting, keeping, and growing employees, taking into consideration generational values, expectations, and behaviors.

n-gen People Performance Inc. is a performance consulting company that improves metrics in the areas of recruitment, orientation, retention, talent management, and succession planning. The managing partners, Giselle Kovary and Adwoa K. Buahene, have provided consulting services and training workshops to a diverse range of organizations and managers, the focus being on how to layer on a generational perspective to people strategies and how to demonstrate organizational engagement. This book is a culmination of their research and client work, revealing what works and what doesn't. As a result of reading this book, you will have in-depth knowledge of how to create *integrated* people strategies that target all four generations while demonstrating organizational engagement.

We have grouped the employee life cycle—recruitment, orientation, retention, talent management, and succession planning—into three sections:

"How to Get 'Em"   recruitment and orientation

"How to Keep 'Em"   total rewards programs, recognition, and employee brand promises

"How to Grow 'Em"   career-pathing, learning and development, mentoring, performance management, succession planning, and management practices

In each section, we link generational identities with strategies, policies, and programs that motivate your multigenerational workforce. We also provide guidance on how your organization should demonstrate the characteristics of organizational engagement.

This book can be read in whole or used as a reference guide in part. We would recommend reading all chapters as each section of the employee life cycle is intimately connected. At minimum, we recommend that you read "Section I: Setting the Stage" prior to reading any other section. The subsequent chapters can be read and used discretely. Each chapter has a consistent format ending with a sample checklist that allows you to measure your demonstration of organizational engagement.

Before reviewing the sections, it's important that we make two qualifications.

Qualification 1: Stereotyping Based on Age

The first is our fine legal print. Under no circumstances is n-gen People Performance Inc. recommending, endorsing, supporting, or encouraging the labeling of people simply based on age. It's never acceptable to stereotype an employee. For example, if your employee is a Gen Xer, you *should not* label them as a high-expectation/high-maintenance employee. As a manager, you should seek to understand the characteristics, motivators, and personality of each of your direct reports. However, it is interesting to consider generational identities as one possible lens through which you can understand your employee groups. The research in generational identities has shown that there is enough commonality across a core group of people that allows us to speak of generational identities in a meaningful way. By taking a macro view of your workforce, you can create integrated strategies that engage all four generations.

Qualification 2: Generations and Multiculturalism—
The Relationship

The second qualifier is on the need to pay attention to generational identities as well as ethic diversity. Certainly, our research is from a western perspective based on U.S., Canada, western Europe—Italy, Germany, England, France—as well as Australia. Thus, all those countries that participated heavily in WW II and had a baby boom after the war. Some research also indicates that the generational identities and behaviors are demonstrated similarly in Japan.

Despite this book's western perspective, it remains critical for managers and organizations to address generational gaps as part of creating a diverse workforce for the following reasons:

1. We are not presenting an "either/or" argument for ethnic diversity or generational cohorts. Rather, we are stating it as an "and" argument. We recommend that *both* generational diversity and ethnic diversity be maximized.

2. Corporate and organizational structures, strategies, programs, and policies in North America are built on western Traditionalists and Baby Boomer values. So for immigrants, it's important that they understand the values and behaviors upon which organizations have built their corporate cultures and performance expectations. To be successful in navigating the business environment, it's important to understand the norms that have created our work environments.

3. It may be true that you will have immigrant employees that don't demonstrate the behaviors and characteristics of their age cohort. In these cases, a manager can remove the demographic age brackets associated with each generation, using the data to help identify four different types of employee groups. For example, a twenty-five-year-old immigrant employee

from a traditionalist country may demonstrate all of the values and behaviors of a western Traditionalist over the age to sixty. In this case, it's important that managers recognize and have the ability to create a collaborative team environment. The twenty-five-year-olds from a traditionalist country may not understand their third-generation twenty-five-year-old North American Gen Y colleagues and vice versa. The twenty-five-year-old Gen Ys may wonder why the twenty-five-year-old Traditionalists won't share openly their performance review, salary, and opinion of their manager. The twenty-five-year-old Traditionalists may view the twenty-five-year-old Gen Ys as rude for speaking so openly in meetings and for challenging authority and existing policies. In this example, managers must be able to help each understand the others' identity and manage clash points.

Finally, some research suggests that, in particular, the younger generations may have a stronger affiliation to their age cohort than their ethnic or gender group. So a person might refer to herself as a "young African American woman," thereby placing first allegiance to other *young* people rather than with her ethnic or gender group. According to a *Fortune Magazine* article, for Gen Ys with friends around the globe who are easily accessible by instant communication, this is particularly true.[1]

Section Overview

Section I
Setting the Stage: Today's Employee Mindset and Generational Identities

The first two chapters set the context for the book. Chapter 1 explains the mindset of today's employees. They view themselves as investors, seeking a return on investment (ROI) from their organizations. As investors, they expect a win-win relationship. We will discuss why it matters to getting, keeping, and growing talent that there are four generations. We will also introduce the concept and definition of organizational engagement. We will underscore the need for organizations to demonstrate these characteristics in order to increase employee engagement within a multigenerational workforce.

Chapter 2 dives into generational cohort identities as they relate to behaviors in the workplace. In this chapter, the focus is on how everyday behavior and expectations can lead to clash points between the generations. We categorize these behaviors into five organizational factors: relationship with the organization, relationship with authority, relationship with colleagues, work styles and management styles. The explanation of these five factors will help to clarify many of the root causes for poor team dynamics, performance issues, and productivity losses.

Section II
How to Get 'Em: Recruitment and Orientation Programs

Chapter 3 focuses on recruitment. The five components of a successful recruitment strategy are discussed: use a blended approach, focus on cultural fit, close the gap, leverage the brand, and maximize internal recruitment strategies. We will highlight how to demonstrate organizational engagement in recruiting before layering on the generational identities. To recruit successfully across the four generations, you need to identify your messages and tailor them to each generation. We will answer the following questions: What works in recruitment? What does each generation want to experience in the recruitment process?

Chapter 4 discusses the role of orientation. Recruitment and orientation are so intimately connected that it doesn't make sense to create a recruitment strategy without also creating an orientation strategy. You can work hard to recruit and attract people to your organization, but if you don't seal the psychological deal within the first twelve weeks, your recruitment efforts are in jeopardy. The important components of an orientation program, both formal and informal, are discussed. We will answer the following questions: How do you demonstrate transparency, responsiveness, and partnering in orientation? How do you ensure that you are meeting the needs of all four generations to successfully seal the psychological deal?

Section III
How to Keep 'Em: Total Rewards Programs and Employee Brand Promises

Chapter 5 explores total rewards with a special focus on recognition programs. We will define the principles that support the creation of strong total rewards programs and outline the components. In particular, we will highlight one component—recognition—discussing the features of a successful program. We will answer the following questions: How does each generation rank the value of your total rewards program? How do you demonstrate organizational engagement in total rewards and recognition programs?

Chapter 6 explores the role of employee brand promises in keeping employees. We will define employee brand promises and focus on the need for consistent execution and constant communication. We will answer the following questions: What are the most critical characteristics to successfully design and implement an employee brand promise? What should the objectives be of an employee brand promise in helping to retain a multigenerational workforce?

Section IV
How to Grow 'Em: Career-pathing, Learning and Development, Mentoring, Performance Management, Succession Planning, and Management Practices

Chapter 7 reviews the need and elements required within career-pathing. We will discuss a new concept of spiral career paths. We will also discuss the importance of career-pathing to developing employees. We will answer the following questions: What do career paths look like? How does a robust career-pathing road map help to grow all four generations?

Chapter 8 focuses on learning and development. We will highlight the qualities and importance of learning and development in building your workforce. In particular, we will highlight the need for increased action learning. We will answer the following questions: Why is learning and development a critical component to your business success? What are the generational expectations of learning and development?

Chapter 9 considers the role of mentoring in growing your people. We will contrast the old model of mentoring with a newer, updated version. The relationship between mentor and mentee in the new model of mentoring is more collaborative and free flowing. We will answer the following questions: What does the mentor and the mentee relationship need to look like? What are the generational perceptions of mentoring?

Chapter 10 explores performance management. The goals and qualities of a robust performance management process are framed within the objective of meeting business goals. In particular, we will highlight the increasing need for objectivity within your performance management system. We will answer the following questions: What is the role of the manager and the employee within the performance management process? What is the comfort level of each generation in participating in a robust performance management process?

Chapter 11 outlines our four-point succession planning process. The main focus of this chapter is on a discussion of three succession planning models, which form the foundation of an effective strategy. The models are evaluated based on their ability to align to generational identities and the characteristics of organizational engagement. We will answer the following questions: What is the best succession planning model to address the expectations of all four generations? What are the key elements in creating a robust succession planning process?

Chapter 12 completes the "How to Grow 'Em" section with a discussion of management practices that engage employees. In this chapter, coaching, communication, and collaboration are highlighted as the three critical competencies that must be mastered by all managers. To be effective, managers need to focus on being strong people managers. For each skill, we provide an overview of the content provided in our development programs. We will answer the following questions: Why is being a strong coach, communicator, and collaborator important in developing people? What does each generation expect from their manager?

We conclude the book with a discussion of the future of people strategies. What will organizations in the future need to focus on? What will be the relationship between the future of business and the future of people strategies?

Section I

Setting the Stage

Chapter One

Employee Mindset:
Employees Looking for the Win Win

Employees today are smart, savvy, and shrewd. Whether as an hourly worker or as a salaried employee, workers are more self-empowered and self-sufficient than ever before. It's relatively simple to describe the mindset of employees today. They view themselves as investors, and they expect a win-win employment relationship. In this chapter, we will describe the investor mindset, explaining how it came to be. The demand for a win-win employment relationship is discussed in the context of why employees are able to demand it. Critically, for the purpose of this book, we layer on the generational perspective on to the mindset. By understanding today's employee mindset from a generational perspective, you have the foundational knowledge that allows you to demonstrate transparency, responsiveness, and partnering. These are the characteristics of organizational engagement. Without organizational engagement, you won't drive the level of employee engagement required to maintain your competitive advantage.

Employees as Investors

Most employees no longer view themselves as lucky to have work; rather, they view organizations as lucky to have them. After all, many messages given by organizations support this mindset. Messages such as "Our employees are our greatest asset" or "We value our employees" or "You can build your career here" reinforce the idea that employees are wanted. In the last decade, organizations have continuously emphasized the value that employees bring to an organization; in return, employees now question the value that an organization delivers to them. Even for well-established organizations, the value they deliver to employees is no longer a given.

If employees are considered to be an asset by an organization, then as such they have a certain value. They are an organization's human capital. Human capital (HC) is defined as the sum of ability (knowledge, skill, talent) + behavior x effort x time.[1]

$$HC = ability + behavior \times effort \times time$$

Ability is education, whether formal or on the job, and natural talents. While the value of ability can be increased through further training and performance management systems, its value may not fluctuate as much as behavior, effort, and time. These three components will increase or decrease in value at the discretion of the employee. Organizations can influence the value of this capital. *Abilities* can be developed, *behaviors* can be modified, and *effort* and *time* can be encouraged. When organizations view human capital like any other resource that should be maximized, then the sustainability of human capital becomes an important business objective. The consequence of not properly managing your organization's human capital is higher turnover, loss of key knowledge, and reduced productivity.

Today's employees know that they bring value to your organization. They are investing their human capital with you. Employees no longer view themselves as property of an organization; rather, they are free-market investors. They will move their human capital to organizations that offer them the best ROI. Organizations created this marketplace when they forced employees to be in charge of their own career growth and development.

Because of an increasingly competitive marketplace, management shifted their focus from building a loyal, stable workforce in the late '70s to increasing organizational performance and reducing costs in the '80s.[2] Downsizing and the flattening of management hierarchies resulted in the dismissal of many loyal, long-tenured managers (particularly middle managers). For those employees who were left, organizations made it clear that they could no longer guarantee job security.[3] The assumption that employees will have long-term job security in exchange for unquestioning loyalty was destroyed. Employees who had diligently worked believing that what was good for the organization would be good for them, were left to fend for themselves.[4] In response to those actions, employees reacted by changing how they defined themselves and their relationship with organizations.

Win-Win Employment Relationship

Organizations tore up that *old* implicit (sometimes explicit) employment deal.[5] During the '70s, '80s, and right up to the late '90s, there were more than enough employees with the human capital that organizations needed. However, with the dot-com boom, we began to see what the other side of the equation could look like. In the new reality, people became the competitive advantage.[6] For some organizations, they are not just struggling to find the right person for the job, they struggle to find *any* person to fill the job. Today, employees realize that they are faced with a new employment deal.[7] In this new employment deal, not much is a given; it's an open-ended agreement between an organization and its employees. The deal that is initially negotiated upon hiring is subject to continuous renegotiation by either the employee or the employer. In such a model, the relationship boils down to the basic principles of negotiation, bargaining influence and power.

The employer holds negotiating power with its compensation model, learning and development opportunities, and organizational culture. Employees hold negotiating power with their human capital. If an employee's human capital is at a level that the organization values and desires but the employee doesn't feel that the organizational offer (i.e., compensation and learning opportunity) is satisfactory, then s/he may renegotiate the terms of the employment deal. Conversely, if an employer is not satisfied with the level of an employee's performance, the employer may renegotiate the terms of the employment contract.

While looking at employment in this way may not be novel, what is new is the degree to which employees have adopted and made decisions based on this viewpoint. The employment deal used to be far more one-sided. Employers held most of the power and influence, and employees had a limited scope to negotiate, especially once they began working for an organization. Now, employees are much more vocal when they are not engaged and much more inclined to act upon their discontent. When possible, most employees will try to negotiate a better deal internally first. But if they feel that they can't renegotiate with their manager or the results don't meet their expectations, they will look for another organization who wants their human capital.

There are very practical, simple reasons employees have greater bargaining power than ever before. North America is facing an aging workforce and a shrinking labor pool. In 2006, the first wave of Baby Boomers turned sixty; thousands turn sixty every day.

Labor Shortage

As Baby Boomers exit the workforce, not enough people are entering it. In the United States, the U.S. Bureau of Census states, "Almost 90 percent of the next decade's net increase in the working-age population will occur in the 55 to 64 years age category."[8] As the labor force is aging, North America and parts of Europe are faced with the challenge of not having enough young employees to replace the gap created by retiring employees. The labor force growth rate, defined as the number of people entering the labor force, will peak in 2007 and decline rapidly over the next decade.[9] The Conference Board of Canada states, "[The] steep decline in labor force growth is at the root of the labor supply crisis that will develop in Canada around 2010."

From reading national newspapers and reports and from watching the news, it's clear that there is already a shortage of employees. The level to which that shortage will grow is debatable and difficult to forecast. Many jobs that will become vacant may not need to be replaced because of increased technology and operating efficiencies.

However, there is little doubt that most, if not all, industries will face a period where there will be more jobs than people to fill them.

The United States, with 78 million Baby Boomers, will be hit with mass retirement. One study highlights that among private industry categories, the hardest that will be hit by the shrinking labor pool will be the executive, administrative, and managerial occupations. Those that are forty-five years and older currently make up 41 percent of employees in this group; 42 percent of those workers are expected to retire by 2008.[10] The Bureau of Labor Statistics indicates that in the public sector, education will be significantly impacted by mass retirement, including teachers, administrators, and operational personnel.[11] In the public sector, 59 percent are aged forty-five and older, and 42 percent of public administrators are projected to leave the labor market by 2008. Other functions that are going to be in hot demand include management analysts, social workers, industrial engineers, postal clerks, police supervisors, detectives, and financial managers.[12]

With 9.6 million Baby Boomers in Canada, certain industries and certain skill/function levels will be impacted by the labor shortage sooner than others. The impact of retirements are being felt in both public and private industries; the shortage is occurring in the public sector where retirement occurs earlier (on average at fifty-eight years old), followed by the private sector where people tend to retire at the age of sixty-two.[13] Numerous federal departments have admitted that they may lose between 50 to 80 percent of middle managers and senior leaders as they will be eligible for retirement in the next three to five years. The industrial sectors, including construction and manufacturing, are already facing mass retirement. Additionally, the list of functions that will be affected include, but are not limited to, senior management, engineers, technicians, geologists, mechanics, equipment operators, software engineers, surgeons, nurses, pharmacists, financial planners, accountants, and undertakers.[14] Individual reports, market data, and labor trends all point to the fact that we are quickly heading into a demand-side labor market.

The combination of scarcity of labor with scarcity of skills means lost opportunities and reduced competitiveness for organizations. A U.S. Bureau of

Labor Statistics economist stated that the implications could also be enormous. In those industries where technology cannot replace human effort, such as health services and education, "service could suffer and needs could go unmet."[15] Even in those industries where innovative technology could lessen the number of employees required, the technology is often complex and complicated, therefore requiring long periods of training, both on and off the job, before employees are up to speed. Regardless of the best efforts of labor-saving technology and immigration, a labor shortage of 4 to 6 million employees is estimated by 2010.[16]

As the Conference Board states, "Without a secure pool of talented workers, many industries and trades are predicting a difficult future, and some companies are already unable to undertake major projects because of labor and skill shortages. Many firms are afraid that the price of skill shortages will be reduced competitiveness and ultimately their very existence may be threatened."[17] The Conference Board has conducted a comprehensive study that forecasts a labor shortage in Canada of almost 1 million workers by 2020. The study states, "[The] dimensions of the problem are enormous, and a growing difficulty in hiring or retaining existing employees will dramatically alter the structure of the Canadian labor markets."[18]

Many of the at-risk occupations are either entirely or partly comprised of knowledge workers. It is this category of workers who individually may be the toughest negotiator in the employment deal. Knowledge workers have "high levels of skills/education with technological literacy, high cognitive power, and abstract reasoning."[19] Our economies and complex organizations rely on these types of employees to produce effective actions and solutions. Without these employees, organizations won't remain competitive.

In a marketplace where there is a greater demand than supply, the employment deal shifts to one in which organizations are willing to give greater concessions in order to create a longer-term employment relationship. Employers also have to be open to renegotiate existing employment terms with existing employees. Organizations that can strike the best win-win employment deal for all employee groups will not only win the recruitment and retention game, but will also succeed in creating the highest levels of employee engagement.

Generational Considerations

How quickly and intensely employees demonstrate to your organization that they are equal bargaining partners or free-market investors can depend on their generational cohort. All generational cohorts value having a positive relationship with their manager. We don't disagree with such a claim. However, we argue that there is a difference in the degree to which each generation values or places weight on that characteristic. The difference isn't in wanting or not wanting a great relationship with a manager. The difference between the generations is the degree and intensity to which a generation responds to, adopts, or rejects this value. For example, while Baby Boomers desire good relationships with their managers, they will ive their organizations or their managers a longer grace period than Gen Xers or Gen Ys to get that relationship right. The younger generations expect a positive relationship from day one of employment. Gen Xers and Gen Ys place such a high value on their relationship with their manager that they give an organization and its managers only a matter of months (if not weeks) to get the relationship right. Traditionalists or Baby Boomers place greater value on working for a strong organization or team, so they will tolerate a poor manager-employee relationship longer.

The need to understand the four generational cohorts becomes increasingly important as the labor market shifts from the supply side to the demand side. How hard candidates and existing employees negotiate their employment deal may depend on their generational cohort identity. Traditionalists and Baby Boomers will often negotiate within the framework that they experienced for the last few decades of work. They were accustomed to a marketplace with high levels of competition and great labor supply. They are more likely to seek employment based on where they believe they can add value to the organization. Gen Xers, and in particular Gen Ys, will negotiate with a level of intensity that might seem cold and calculating. They are more demanding about negotiating an employment deal that will benefit them. They view the relationship as short term and more contractual; for these cohorts, employment is just business.

Defining Organizational and Employee Engagement

Ultimately, the goal of understanding the generational identities and how they respond to the employment deal is to increase levels of employee engagement. Employee engagement is different from employee satisfaction. Satisfaction measures how happy or content employees are with your organization, its policies and practices, and their jobs. Research has been inconclusive in finding a direct correlation between productivity and high levels of employee satisfaction—though the assumption has been that there is a positive link.[20] Engagement refines the link between employee attitudes/behaviors and productivity. Engagement measures whether employees actually *do more* because they are engaged. Most of the literature and research about engagement, produced mainly by national and global HR consulting houses, focuses on the qualities of an engaged employee.[21] Despite minor variations, they all agree that employees demonstrate engagement through a rational and emotional connection to your organization. Rationally, engaged employees expend discretionary effort; emotionally, they say good things about your organization internally and externally.

Expending discretionary effort means giving that little extra, working at the 110 percent level more frequently. Most employees that expend their discretionary effort are part of your high-potential employee pool, especially if they also feel emotionally connected to your organization. They speak highly of your organization to their friends, families, and strangers. Being emotionally connected is crucial to being an engaged employee. While some employees may not expend discretionary effort, they may remain emotionally connected to your organization. These employees still meet and perhaps exceed performance targets and expectations. However, once the emotional connection is lost, employees mentally "check out." Employees that are no longer emotionally connected to your organization either quit and leave or, worse yet, stay and continue working but are actively disengaged from your organization.

We agree with the two popular characteristics of an engaged employee, discretionary effort and emotional connection, but we believe a third quality needs to be included. An engaged employee also demonstrates acceptance of accountability. Accepting accountability is a hybrid between an emotional and rational quality. Employees accept accountability when they feel that they have trust in your organization. When employees believe they are in a safe environment, where they are empowered and risk taking is encouraged, they accept accountability. For example, you know you have created a culture where accountability is accepted when employees initiate project reviews and determine what could/should be done differently without focusing on laying blame. For engaged employees, there is little need to point fingers unless they are ready to point a finger at themselves as well. They acknowledge accountability within their own job, as well as demonstrating accountability for the success of their departments and the organization as a whole. Employees that accept accountability do so for activities that fall outside of their job description. They take on activities or tasks that are beyond their role to ensure that corporate, department, and team goals are met.

Characteristics of an Engaged Organization	Characteristics of an Engaged Employee
Transparent	Discretionary Effort
Responsive	Emotionally Connected
Partnering	Accepts Accountability

At n-gen, we don't just measure and evaluate the qualities of an engaged employee; we focus on what your organization should do to demonstrate organizational engagement. Our definition of engagement is *a productive relationship between an organization and its employees.*

ENGAGEMENT
A productive relationship between an organization and its employees

The word *relationship* means that there are two parties involved in the relationship. The word *productive* means that not only should the end result be productive, but also the intrinsic functioning of the relationship. By *organization*, we are not referring just to the executive office, but also to the managers. For most employees, their immediate manager is the embodiment of the organization, regardless of the manager's level within the organization.[22] There are three characteristics that an organization must demonstrate to prove that it is invested in creating a productive relationship with employees—*transparency*, *responsiveness*, and *partnering*.

Transparent means an organization and its leaders are open, honest, and forthcoming with information. Motives and intentions (vision and mission) are clear and consistently communicated to the broadest audience possible. A transparent organization shares information with all levels within the organization and highlights how individual roles, responsibilities, and accountabilities fit into the big picture. *Responsive* means that an organization actively listens to its employee groups and is committed to taking action in a timely manner. A responsive organization communicates what it can and cannot do to meet employee expectations. The organization and its managers proactively manage expectations. *Partnering* means that an organization recognizes that employees are equal partners and investors in the organization. In negotiating and maintaining the employment deal, the organization and its managers seek a win-win relationship with their employees. Also, an organization that partners with employees has managers who view themselves as part of the team, not outside of it.

In building engagement, your organization should consider how you demonstrate the characteristics of organizational engagement to all employee groups. The question to be asked is, would each generation believe that your organization is demonstrating transparency, responsiveness, and partnering? This question applies to all strategies, programs, and policies within the employee life cycle.

The n-gen Engagement Model

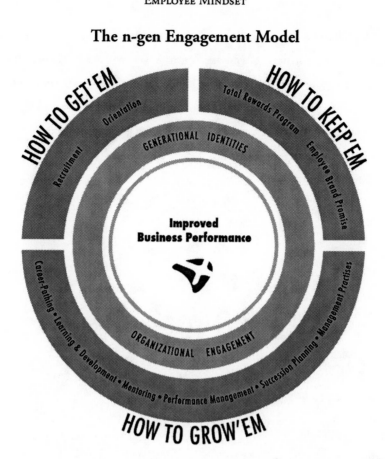

By demonstrating the three characteristics of organizational engagement, you will be setting the stage for greater employee engagement.[23] The qualities of organizational engagement will be the measuring stick with which you will be able to assess your HR strategies, programs, and policies. The objective is to ensure that your solutions align with the generational identities and create the most engaged environment possible.

So the stage has been set. We work in a new world order where employees expect a win-win employment deal with your organization. Only with such an arrangement can organizations drive productivity through higher levels of engagement. However, as you will discover in the following chapters, to demonstrate transparency, responsiveness, and partnering as an organization, you will need to take generational identities into account. By understanding and tapping into generational identities, you will be able to *get, keep, and grow* your human capital. The following chapters focus on layering on the characteristics of organizational engagement and generational identities onto the design of successful people strategies.

Chapter Two

Generational Identities in the Workplace

Given that employees hold a greater bargaining chip, there is an increased need for organizations to create an engaged relationship with all employee groups. To get, keep, and grow the best employees, it is critical to understand your employee markets: who they are, what they want and expect from your organization, and how they differ from one another.

Today's workplace is comprised of four generations:

Traditionalists	1922-1945
Baby Boomers	1946-1964
Gen Xers	1965-1980
Gen Ys	1981-2000

Generational cohorts possess unique values, characteristics, and skills based on their experiences of life-defining events. The commonality of experiences creates generational identities. The generational identities are the viewpoints that each cohort has on life, love, family, work, politics, and society.

Much has been published about the descriptors of each generation, specifically their attitudes and values. Popular media regularly profile how the generational identities differ. For more information about generational identities, please read the appendix, which describes in detail each cohort's life-defining events, characteristics,

and values. The appendix provides a sociological context for why the viewpoints
held by each generational cohort exist. In this chapter, we will focus on describing
how generational identities translate into behaviors in the workplace. Generational
behaviors are important to understand because they impact individual, team, and
organizational performance. This focus on workplace behaviors is new and most
relevant to your organization in achieving top performance.

What's a Generation?

The most comprehensive approach to defining a generation is to use both
demography and sociology. Demographers typically define a generation according
to the rise and fall of birth rates, giving us the term *Baby Boomers* for those born
post-World War II. Sociologists examine the critical life-defining events that affect
a generation's collective identity. These life-defining events are profound because
they occur at a time when a generation is young enough to be malleable and
psychologically influenced.[1] Cohorts are bound together by a shared coming-of-age
period. Psychologists remind us that our core values are programmed during our
first fifteen to sixteen years of life, through a combination of five major life-shaping
influences such as parent/family; schools/education, religion/morality, friends/peers,
and media/culture. It is during this time also that major political, social, and/or
economic events create a common history and connection with others of the same
age. The decisions we make in our professional and personal lives are rooted in our
value systems, which were formed long before we got our driver's license.[2] We may still
mature and change throughout the years, but most of our core values remain intact.

The Four Generations Demographics: North America

	United States[3]			
	Traditionalist	**Baby Boomer**	**Gen X**	**Gen Y**
Total	48.7 million	78.3 million	63.3 million	80.4 million
% of Population[4]	17%	28%	23%	29%

	Canada[5]			
	Traditionalist	Baby Boomer	Gen X	Gen Y
Total	5.2 million	9.6 million	6.7 million	8.3 million
% of Population[6]	16%	30%	21%	26%

Impact of Demographics on the Workplace

With four generations in the workplace, organizations are faced with four different, and often conflicting, approaches to work. As each generation has its own unique identity, their "generational baggage" travels with them into the workplace, impacting team, departmental, and organizational performance. For example, when a traditionalist's respect for authority and directive management style meets a Gen Xer's relaxed attitude toward authority and informal work style, conflicts can erupt between team members. When generational approaches to work clash, the results are increased turnover, reduced employee engagement, and diminished business results. As we discussed in chapter 1, there are commonalities among the values, expectations, and behaviors of the four generations. The differences among the generations are either definitional in nature or are demonstrated in the degree and intensity that a generation emphasizes a particular value, behavior, or expectations. Each cohort's identity translates into behaviors in the workplace. We have grouped these behaviors and termed them organizational factors. It is through these factors that you can clearly see where generational differences and potential clash points might occur.

The five organizational factors are the following:

1. Relationship with the organization
2. Relationship with authority
3. Relationship with colleagues
4. Work styles
5. Management styles

Relationship with the Organization: *Pay Your Dues versus What Dues Are You Paying Me?*

Whether or not employee loyalty exists today is a hotly debated topic. Some believe that employees broke the deal by no longer committing to an organization over the long term. However, as we have discussed in chapter 1, we argue that loyalty ceased to exist because organizations did not keep their end of the bargain. A study of CEOs and business leaders, it was noted that 59 percent of respondents believe that younger employees are less loyal because their employers are no longer loyal toward them. One of their comments included the following:

> There is no question that massive layoffs in various sectors have contributed to employees' perceptions regarding the lack of corporate loyalty. Most companies have followed an all-or-nothing approach. Only a handful have tried to work with employees to keep them on through job sharing, retraining, etc.[7]

CEO's ranked loyalty of younger employees (those under thirty years old) as very low compared to thirty years ago. Eighty percent of respondents ranked employee loyalty below the midpoint of 4 on a 7-point scale, where 7 represented "a lot more loyal" and 1 represented "a lot less loyal."[8] Regardless of who decided to be less loyal first, the traditional notion of loyalty is virtually non-existent in many workplaces. Certainly, if we define loyalty in traditional terms—an employee gives to an organization with the expectation of life-long employment and cradle-to-grave job security—then loyalty is dead. Loyalty must now be defined by the actions and behaviors demonstrated by both the organization and employees and not based on years of service or tenure.

The following chart describes at which level within an organization each generation places their loyalty, what expectations they hold regarding their work, and the behaviors they demonstrate.

Relationship with the Organization

	Traditionalists	Boomers	Gen Xers	Gen Ys
Definition	Loyal to the organization	Loyal to the team	Loyal to the manager	Loyal to colleagues
Behaviors And Expectations	Has long term commitment and tenure	Add value by going that extra mile	Exceed expectations and deliver results	Ensure equitable treatment
	Career = opportunity	Career = self worth	Career = one part of me	Career = opportunity to add value and contribute
	Pay-your-dues mentality	Live-to-work mentality	Work-to-live mentality	Work-to-contribute mentality
	Climb the corporate ladder based on tenure	Fight your way up the corporate ladder	Focus on your professional ladder—the corporate ladder might get pulled away	The corporate ladder is a spiral staircase

Not surprisingly, Traditionalists tend to be loyal to an organization at an organizational level. They feel tied to an organization regardless of how competent their leaders or managers might be. Sometimes referred to as being loyal to a fault, this generation expects to build a life-long career with one employer or at least within one industry. When Traditionalists entered the workplace, they did so with an expectation that they would "work hard from nine to five, pay their dues, and be loyal to the company. In return they received a decent wage, lifetime employment, and pensions when they retired."[9] Job hopping was viewed as being disloyal. An employee who made a commitment to an organization was expected to stay in the organization for life. Traditionalists view their careers as an opportunity to leave a legacy and contribute to something bigger than themselves. It is for this reason that Traditionalists are interested in working on long-standing projects that will have an impact at an organizational level.

Baby Boomers initially entered the workplace with similar expectations as those of Traditionalists. They assumed that they would work for only a handful of employers and that they would likely stay within the same profession. Though initially loyal to an organization, downsizing caused many Baby Boomers to shift their loyalty to the team (meaning their department). By being on the star team, they could individually be stars themselves. As a result of this type of team player mentality, organizations sometimes ended up with competing departmental silos, each aiming to be the star team on an initiative. Well-known for their workaholic tendencies, this generation has gone that extra mile to demonstrate their commitment and loyalty to the team. The long work hours and the pressure to be a team player meant that Baby Boomers typically view their careers as a defining characteristic of their self-worth. For Boomers, their profession and career path defines who they are to themselves and others.

Gen Xers place their loyalty at the manager level because it is the manager who is the gatekeeper to their success. A manager decides what learning opportunities, stretch assignments, cross-functional projects, and promotions Gen Xers can access. Great managers are the single most important people to Gen X employees. This cohort cares little about which organization they work for or even which department they belong to. What they do care about is whether or not they can create a win-win, collaborative relationship with their manager. Gen Xers view loyalty to their manager as a two-way street. They demonstrate loyalty by exceeding expectations and delivering results; in return, they expect managers to commit to their development through learning and development and challenging work assignments. When Gen Xers find good managers, they hold on to them with all their might, often following them from department to department or organization to organization. Gen Xers view their career as only one part of who they are. With a live-to-work mentality, the members of this generation are equally focused on other aspects of their lives, like their personal lives, hobbies, and life-long learning. Most Gen Xers anticipate that they will be downsized at some point in their career, so they have committed to making work only one part of their identity.

Similar to Baby Boomers, Gen Ys are interested in working as part of a team. However, this cohort places their loyalty with their colleagues across functions. Gen Ys demonstrate loyalty to their peer group by ensuring that each cohort member is treated equitably. This cohort desires a workplace culture where they can work with their friends and where the organization demonstrates a commitment to them as a collective group. We know of a Gen Y nurse who turned down an opportunity for full-time employment until the rest of her colleagues could also receive the same employment option. The tendency for Gen Ys to move in packs strongly influences this cohort's short—and long-term commitments. Gen Ys view their careers as an opportunity to add value regardless of how long they may be employed at your organization. There is no internal struggle of commitment to an organization, team, or manager. While they are at your organization, Gen Ys want to work and contribute; they will commit as long as the employment relationship lasts. The length of your relationship with them depends on their perceptions of how meaningful the work is and the type of contribution they can make. After all, they have been continuously told that they will have lots of different careers with lots of different employers, so why would they commit only to you?

Generational Clash Points

Michael is a Gen X employee with a large financial services firm. He has been employed there for two years and has always received strong performance reviews. Michael has recently signed up for a photography course on Thursday nights. He's interested in learning more about his favorite hobby as he has already been hired to do some shoots for friends' weddings. He is considering starting a photography business on the side. Michael is also an avid kickboxer and is training for an upcoming competition. Michael regularly leaves work early on Tuesdays and Thursdays to make it to his kickboxing and photography classes. While he always meets his deliverables, some of Michael's baby boomer colleagues and his boss question his loyalty to the organization and the team. They regularly work late to finish up projects and sacrifice their own personal lives for the benefit of the organization. They don't understand Michael's relaxed attitude toward work and aren't sure if he is really committed to his job or the success of the team. If he is so focused on other interests and hobbies, how can he be serious about his career? Michael knows that some of his colleagues take note of when he's leaving early—they check their watches as he walks out or make comments about how late they worked the night before. This doesn't bother Michael because he places a greater value on a work-life balance than on impressing his colleagues or boss. He's mystified that his colleagues would make their careers the most important aspect of their lives at the expense of a more fulfilling personal life. Frequently, Michael works from home in the evenings and responds to important business issues, but he doesn't feel a need to communicate this to others. From his point of view, it's none of their business how he manages his work as long as he gets the job done on time and within budget. He believes he has a very strong work ethic even if others don't perceive it the same way. For him, it's about achieving results, not just putting in long hours.

Relationship with Authority: *Dear Ms. CEO, Here Is How I Think We Could Improve the Company*

In conjunction with a shift in loyalty, the workplace of today is also characterized by change in how employees view those in positions of authority. Historically, expertise, age, or status accorded a person respect. Children were taught to respect their elders and people in positions of authority. Today, how we define authority has changed, particularly in the workplace. Authority is no longer simply based on tenure, experience, or age. As we have moved from a tenure-based to a competency-based organizational structure, authority is now granted based on performance and skill set. The following chart describes how each generation defines respect for authority, the expectations they have of their relationship with authority, and the behaviors they demonstrate.

Relationship with Authority

	Traditionalists	Boomers	Gen Xers	Gen Ys
Definition	Respect authority and hierarchical system	Challenge authority	Unimpressed by authority	Respect authority who demonstrate competence
Behaviors And Expectations	Formal relationships with superiors Seniority and job titles are respected Tell me what I should do for you	Personal relationships with superiors Desire for flat organizations that are democratic Let me show you what I can do for you	Informal relationships with superiors Competence and skills are respected over seniority Tell me what you can do for me	Casual relationships with superiors Traditional path flipped by possessing specific competencies Show me what you can do for me right now

Given their acceptance of a hierarchical-based system, Traditionalists respect authority based on title and level within an organization. Respect is bestowed regardless of personal traits. Expertise is assumed by the level of accomplishment; if you are a director, vice president, or CEO, you must know what you're doing. This type of respect is also demonstrated by having formal relationships with superiors. Traditionalists fully expect to be handed work or projects by their manager and don't expect to be asked how they feel about working on a certain task. The boss is the boss, and you do what you're told—until, of course, you become the boss, and then you get your chance to tell others what to do.

Baby Boomers entered the work environment with anti-establishment attitudes and a tendency to challenge authority. However, given the competitive nature of the workplace, many Baby Boomers had to mellow their expectations and conform to a hierarchical way of working. They understood that in a competitive environment, it is best to align yourself with the right people, so Boomers' political savvy and team orientation leads them to become far friendlier with superiors than Traditionalists. They will socialize, go for drinks after work, attend all corporate and industry functions, and network whenever possible. Today, as Boomers assume responsibility for senior leadership positions, they have influenced the work environment to be more collaborative, democratic, and consensus building.

Given the skeptical nature of Gen Xers, they are completely unimpressed with authority for authority's sake. For this cohort, tenure or title holds little value in and of itself. Tenure or title doesn't automatically translate into expertise or skills. From the Gen Xer's perspective, managers who have risen through the ranks aren't necessarily good at their jobs or engaged in what they do. What is respected is competency and skills. For the younger generations, respect is given to those who demonstrate exceptional performance and who are willing to help them develop their own skill sets by passing on knowledge and expertise. Challenging authority is not seen as disrespectful or rude. By viewing the employment relationship as an equal partnership, the younger generations believe that they have a right to provide feedback and comments up the organization as much as senior managers have a right to provide direction in a downward manner. Gen Xers tend to be rather informal with superiors. They demonstrate the same level of familiarity with their colleagues as they do with their manager, director, or CEO.

Like Gen Xers, Gen Ys reject having to give respect to authority based solely on tenure or title because many Gen Ys have been raised in peer-to-peer relationships at home, valuing egalitarianism. They view everyone, regardless of position or title, as a colleague—including senior management and, therefore, expect that they can interact with senior people in a casual, relaxed way. At one organization during a town hall meeting, a Gen Y employee realized that the CEO lived in his neighborhood. He was thrilled and stated, "Cool! We can come to work together."

In many instances, Gen Ys have flipped the traditional model of hierarchy that is aligned to years of experience on its head. With the rise of information technology, many Gen Ys enter the workplace in a position of authority because they possess specialized competencies. Since most organizations have moved to a competency, result-focused structure, it's not unusual to see younger employees in senior positions earlier in their careers. They may be more senior within an organization despite fewer years of work. And frequently, they are managing employees who are older than themselves and who have more on-the-job experience than they do.

Generational Clash Points

Lindsay, a Gen Y, has just been hired by a midsize marketing firm. She is fresh out of college and is eager to contribute and add value to the organization. Within her first week on the job, Lindsay encounters a situation where she disagrees with her manager's decision to eliminate promotions via text messaging as part of a client's marketing strategy. She sends her manager Gail an e-mail stating her opinion and offers a suggestion on how things could be changed. She challenges Gail to explain why she made the decision that she did and what data she has to support her decision. Lindsay is proud that she took the initiative; after all, she has always been encouraged to give her opinion and to speak up if she disagrees. Gail is shocked. She can't believe how disrespectful her new employee is. She has only been at work for one week and already she wants to change things. Gail can't imagine a time when she would have questioned her manager's authority like that, especially not within the first few months of working! When Lindsay doesn't receive a reply to her e-mail within a few hours, she assumes that Gail has ignored her comments. So she forwards her e-mail to the VP of Marketing who she met last week in her orientation program. He was a very nice man, and said that if she had any questions, she could contact him. The VP is even more taken aback by Lindsay's e-mail. He wonders why she hadn't resolved this issue directly with Gail. He doesn't expect to get involved in discussions of this nature and asks Gail to handle this situation. Gail feels both embarrassed that he was involved and frustrated that she needs to defend and justify her decision to such a new recruit. Her fifteen years of experience in this business should be enough credibility to warrant any decision she makes. Both the VP and Gail worry that they might have a very difficult employee on their hands.

Relationship with Colleagues: *We Work Together, We Play Together, We Start a Business Together*

Considering how the relationship between employers and employees has been redefined, it's interesting to also explore how the relationship between colleagues has changed to reflect a more collaborative, social work environment. In multigenerational teams, colleagues respond differently to one another based on their generational identities. Within the range of possible relationships at work, from formal to informal, each generation intersects at a different point on this continuum. The following chart describes how each generation defines their relationship with colleagues, their expectations of a work relationship, and how they respond to conflict.

Relationship with Colleagues

	Traditionalists	Boomers	Gen Xers	Gen Ys
Definition	Formal relationships	Personal relationships	Friendly Relationships	Casual and social relationships
Behaviors And Expectations	No socialization out of work	Socialization through networking events—business and personal-focused	Socialization through non-work related activities	Socialization at work-sponsored events and non-work related activities
	When in conflict, defer to seniority	Avoid conflict	Open dialogue to resolve conflict	Debate and challenge each other to achieve compromise

Traditionalists tend to keep their personal lives and work lives separate. Other than the company holiday party or family BBQ, members of this cohort rarely socialize with their colleagues outside of work, especially not those more junior or senior to them. Relationships in the workplace are formal. Given their strong sense of structure, when team conflict arises, Traditionalists will defer to authority to make the final decision. Within teams, those with greater seniority are expected to take on a leadership role by setting the direction for the team.

Baby Boomers are well-known for their ability to work in teams in a collaborative and democratic way. As such, Baby Boomers seek personal relationships with their colleagues as a way of strengthening team dynamics. Team building activities often include colleagues revealing something personal as a way of making a deeper connection or participating in experiential activities designed to increase trust on a one-on-one basis. Given the long hours and commitment Boomers invest in their careers, they want to be a part of a team where they can work hard and play hard together. Perhaps as a result of increased personal connections, baby boomer colleagues tend to avoid conflict. They often put on a happy face even if they're in disagreement. When faced with interpersonal challenges as part of a team, Baby Boomers avoid dealing with the root causes of issues in an effort to keep everyone happy. This trait can lead to divisions within a team and the formation of cliques.

Gen Xers approach their relationships with colleagues in a very straightforward way. If they like the people they are working with, they form friendships that extend beyond the workplace, often remaining in touch long after one or the other moves on to a new organization. In the workplace, they create a social network. Outside of work, Gen Xers socialize together on evenings and weekends, but rarely discuss work issues. On the flip side, if colleagues on a team don't click, Gen Xers interact with one another in a very matter-of-fact way, focusing on project tasks and results, caring less about building a personal bond. When team conflict arises, Gen Xers are quick to discuss issues in a straightforward manner in an effort to arrive at a resolution rapidly. In many cases, Gen X team members are very direct and blunt with their feedback to colleagues and their manager, regardless of seniority. For this cohort, disagreement and debate are not personal attacks, but simply a way to overcome obstacles and achieve results.

Gen Ys have a propensity to move in packs. As such, their relationships with colleagues are strong, casual, and social. This generation is eager to work at the same organization as their friends. Perhaps because they are so connected, this cohort shares information freely with colleagues. They discuss performance reviews, salaries, and opinions of their manager. They use technology to stay connected with colleagues and friends during and outside of business hours. Based on their experiences within the school system, Gen Ys are accustomed to debating and challenging one another as a way of achieving a compromise to team conflict. With a strong sense of fair play, this generation ensures that all colleagues are an equal part of the team and are treated in an equitable and egalitarian way.

Generational Clash Points

Walter, a Traditionalist, is part of a multigenerational project team for a large oil and gas company. He has spent twenty years working for the company and clearly understands the organizational culture. However, he has noticed that things are changing. Last week, at a team meeting, some of his younger colleagues were challenging the project manager to explain why they were wasting so much money and time on trying to win a new project. They explained that when they were hanging out together at a baseball game on the weekend, they talked about the fact that their competitor has a much better chance of winning the bid because they have stronger engineering expertise. Also, they know from their colleagues that worked on a similar project for the company last year that these types of projects were late and over budget because of poor management. Walter is shocked that his colleagues would speak about their own organization in such a negative light and would share with one another information about other project teams. The younger employees asked him what he thought. Didn't he also believe it was a waste of time to chase a project they couldn't deliver on? Walter felt uncomfortable being put on the spot and certainly wouldn't make his opinion known publicly. It doesn't matter what he thinks; it's up to the senior leaders to make that decision and to manage the process. Walter isn't sure that everyone should be so open and casual. Shouldn't there still be some discretion?

Work Styles: *I'm Just Stepping Out for a Break, Be Back in Two Hours*

The demonstration of generational differences is most notable in the day-to-day working styles of each cohort. What's considered as a work routine differs from organization to organization. But it may also differ from team to team and individual to individual. Technology—hardware, software, and the Internet—permits each of us to develop unique work routines. This then impacts how we work with others. How we perceive others' work styles is often influenced by our definition of work ethic. Working long hours doesn't necessarily mean someone has a strong work ethic. Just because employees work late in the office doesn't mean they are working harder or smarter. Understanding your organization's culture and perceptions of work style is important to consider in creating a work environment that motivates and engages multigenerational teams. The following chart describes how each generation defines its work style, its expectations of a workplace structure, and how each cohort responds to change.

Work Styles

	Traditionalists	Boomers	Gen Xers	Gen Ys
Definition	Linear	Structured	Flexible	Fluid
Behaviors And Expectations	Follow the rules	Challenge the rules	Change the rules	Create the rules
	Process focused	People focused	Results focused	Technology focused
	Follow the leader	Work in teams	Work independently with little supervision	Work independently with supervision
	Change = something is broken	Change = caution	Change = opportunity	Change = improvement

Linked to the concept of loyalty and dedication, Traditionalists are described as hardworking because of their commitment to get the job done. This cohort is made up of "doers"—those in an organization who ensure projects are completed in adherence to the rules. The members of this generation are less likely than any other to rock the boat or challenge the status quo. Traditionalists are comfortable with a follow-the-leader scenario, where directives are laid out by the manager and executed by the team. Typically, their work style is linear in nature, formal, and process focused. The success of their careers has been built upon creating complex processes and practices for a linear work environment. Traditionalists have a strong sense of personal responsibility toward their work and take pride in an honest day's work for an honest day's pay.

As result of working within a more rigid corporate culture, Traditionalists are often viewed by their colleagues as being resistant to change. Their resistance, however, is not born out of a desire to impede productivity, growth, or innovation. For Traditionalists, change was infrequent in both their personal and professional lives. In fact, change meant that something was wrong. The saying "If it ain't broke, don't fix it" best describes Traditionalists' perceptions of change. For this cohort, change is viewed as a risky move and shouldn't be acted upon quickly. As a result, when organizations make radical shifts, changes are often viewed with concern and apprehension by this cohort. The hesitancy is based on a need to understand how their knowledge and skills will remain valuable to an organization during and after the change. To help in the transition of Traditionalists into new roles, organizational structures, or work processes, managers should reinforce the support they will receive through training, coaching, and additional resources. Managers should also emphasize the value this cohort brings to the ongoing success of your organization.

In opposition to the top-down structure controlled by traditionalist managers, Baby Boomers desire an organizational culture that is more inclusive. Given their belief in equality, this cohort challenged corporate rules to open the door for women, visible minorities, and other subgroups in the workplace. By working collaboratively in teams, Baby Boomers have created workplace cultures that focus on people. They seek consensus and team cohesion. As Baby Boomers have assumed greater responsibility in organizations, their influence on how we work has been significant. Collaborative project teams, strategic alliances, and partnerships are all now commonplace. However, while this cohort created a more flexible workplace culture, their work style is one that still remains highly structured. Baby Boomers remain committed to a typical nine-to-five workday—in fact, most in this generation invest far more time in the office than forty hours per week and are often at the office longer than colleagues from other generations.

This generation is cautious about change for two reasons. First, they have witnessed or have been impacted by corporate downsizing. During this experience, in the '80s and '90s, organizational change was positioned as positive yet had a devastating impact on many Boomers. Secondly, this generation continuously experiences change, personally and professionally, and, therefore, is guarded about new management theories, trends, or strategies. They have witnessed the pendulum swing from one end of the business spectrum to the other—from convergence to divergence, from vertical to horizontal market approaches, have seen and heard it all. Members of this generation have been asked by senior leaders to adopt a variety of management and business ideologies, resulting in professional changes that often didn't achieve the desired results. For this cohort, change can be viewed as positive as long as they are the champion of the change. Organizations should recognize Boomers' initial skepticism to change. Communication that is open, honest, and frequent is the best way to support Boomers through organizational changes.

In contrast to Traditionalists' commitment to following the rules and completing work linearly, Gen Xers approach work from a result-focused standpoint. For this cohort, results are what matter, not process or rules. Driven by a desire to remain marketable, they know that the best way to prove their value to an organization (or prospective employer) is to show output, the numbers they have been able to increase or decrease. For this cohort, it is unimportant where and when they do their work as long as the work gets done on time, in scope, and on budget. Also, as the early adopters of technology, this generation was quick to learn how to multitask. This impacts their work style in that Gen Xers like to work on multiple projects simultaneously in a flexible manner—moving from one to another seamlessly. This flexible work style is well suited to contractual or project-based work where Gen Xers can take on multiple projects, manage their own timelines, and fit work within the mosaic of other personal activities. For Gen Xers, it's not uncommon to take several hours off work during the day to go to the gym or run errands because they're prepared to spend several hours at night working. For this cohort, a flexible time schedule allows them to maintain a work-life balance.

Unlike Baby Boomers who seek consensus when working as part of a team, Gen Xers prefer to work independently. They want freedom and flexibility over how they complete their tasks. Gen Xers' idea of team collaboration is coming together to identify project objectives and outcomes and then going away to work independently on their respective tasks. Given Gen Xers strong focus on results, this cohort is often perturbed with consensus-focused meetings designed to allow team members to discuss project issues in detail. This cohort, with their strong sense of independence, desires that they be able to complete their work with little supervision.

Because they are children of divorced, blended, and dual-working-parent households and because they grew up during difficult economic times, Gen Xers are at ease with change. They are accustomed to adapting to new situations and dealing with ambiguity both in their personal and professional lives. While they may be initially skeptical of managerial and organizational motives, they will adopt change initiatives quickly when they understand what's in it for them. Changes at work mean potential opportunities. A restructuring means that things might be shaken up, and there may be new opportunities, assignments, or positions for Gen Xers.

As the youngest entrants into the workforce, Gen Ys have further advanced Gen Xers' campaign for a work-life balance. Gen Ys are growing up in a world where everything is accessible 24/7. They have never known a world where they can't access money via an ATM, shop at a twenty-four-hour grocery store, or research information online anywhere, anytime. Gen Ys have a fluid work style, where life and work blend together seamlessly. To them, a day no longer needs to be blocked into work time and playtime; professional and personal activities can overlap within the day. Being even more techno-literate than Gen Xers, Gen Ys look to improve workplace efficiency and achieve results by maximizing technology. Since they can do work from their BlackBerry or Treo at any time, they don't see the need to be stuck in the office just to satisfy corporate appearances. Many managers who are accustomed to employees who follow the rules are overwhelmed by Gen Ys' challenging of traditional workplace structures such as formal work hours and time spent on-site rather than time spent remotely accessing work online. While this generation seeks freedom from the traditional structures of a workday, they desire more supervision and direction from their manager than Gen Xers. This apparent contradiction is often difficult for managers to appreciate and manage. It requires a fine balance between providing up-front direction and parameters on a project and then stepping back and letting Gen Ys apply their own creativity to the process. This generation's desire to create new rules and new ways of doing things can have both a positive and negative impact in the workplace.

This generation thrives on change and views it as an integral part of a dynamic workplace. Change has been constant for them. New technology is updated every three to six months, and Gen Ys are often the first to adopt the latest trend. Change means things become better and faster. For this cohort, if a process in your organization has remained the same for twelve months, they think it's probably out of date. They believe technology is the answer to most problems and, therefore, will first look to technology to provide the quickest solution. Not only will Gen Ys embrace change, they can act as fantastic change agents. They can spark innovation throughout your organization by participating on committees that challenge old ways of doing business, pushing the boundaries of your current workplace thinking.

Generational Clash Points

Susan, a Baby Boomer, is a senior account manager at a large manufacturing company. She likes her job and knows what needs to get done to be successful in her role. Her colleague Max, a Gen Xer, is also an account manager and has been with the company for a few years. While Susan likes Max, she can't understand his work habits. He never seems to finish a task before moving on to another one and rarely engages others to help problem solve. While Susan wants to achieve results, she is also respectful of the processes, structures, and policies which she needs to adhere to. Max challenges each step of a process. He doesn't understand why it's so important to follow procedures when from his point of view, most of the steps could be cut out. That way, he could achieve his result faster and more efficiently without all the red tape. Cynthia, a new hire, is a junior account manager and is even more impatient than Max. She doesn't just want to skip steps in a process, but she wants to completely reinvent the process. While some of her ideas are good, Susan doesn't think everything needs to be changed. Most of the time, the existing processes work very well. Even Max agrees that not every process can be changed all the time. On the other hand, Cynthia can't believe that most of the tasks she needs to do to complete a client transaction are still done manually. She expected that such a successful company would be more innovative and techno-savvy. She doesn't understand why Susan, and even Max sometimes, are so reluctant to make improvements to the way work is done. If more processes could be completed online, in real time, then everyone could have a more flexible workday. She wouldn't have to be in the office all the time and attend so many meetings. They could chat via text and make decisions a lot quicker. That would be a lot more fun and efficient.

Management Styles: *Don't Manage Me the Way You Were Managed*

There are often differences between how each generation wants to be managed and how they manage others. How best to manage people has been written about for decades; however, there is a default management style for managers, especially if they haven't been developed into strong people leaders. For many, this default setting is a command-and-control model because it is often the management style they experienced. Helping managers to demonstrate a more collaborative and engaging management style is pivotal in getting, keeping, and growing top talent. The following chart describes how each generation defines its management style, their expectations of direct reports, and how they manage others.

Management Styles

	Traditionalists	Boomers	Gen Xers	Gen Ys
Definition	Command and control	Participative	Collaborative	Hyper collaborative (TBD)
Behaviors And Expectations	Rigid Do what I say, not what I do Micromanagement	Political Do what we've all agreed upon Flavor-of-the-month management—newest trend	Straightforward Do what we need to do to get results Performance-based management	Personal Do what each of us is best at and wants to do Just-in-time management

North American organizational culture was built on a hierarchical model of command-and-control management. Traditionalists who experienced this model at home, in the school system, and in the workplace tend to rely on this approach when leading others. This management style is rigid and focuses on compliance. A good employee is one who doesn't question a manager or challenge his/her authority, especially in a public forum. A hierarchical-based manager demands respect from others without necessarily demonstrating the same level of respect toward them. They control their teams by micromanaging project details as a way of ensuring that they have intimate knowledge of all aspects of a project. They are the leader whom everyone follows without question or reservation. As the most senior authority, they dictate the organization's or team's direction, strategy, and plans. From the top-down, all other managers demonstrate the same behavior, limited to their scope of control based on title and level in the organization. While this management style has been diluted in the past few decades to include a greater level of dialogue and team collaboration, many managers still use a degree of command and control to manage their teams.

Baby Boomers wanted to create a workplace where more voices could be heard. The challenge they faced in implementing this organizational change was that traditional leaders were unwilling to surrender decision-making control to others. A command-and-control system is a comfortable model for managers because control remains in their hands. As Baby Boomers experienced career growth and began to assume management positions, they struggled to influence organizational culture and to create their own management style. Boomers prefer to be managed by managers that are participatory and seek consensus. Yet, while they desire this alternative management style, they have difficulty implementing changes to their own approach. Unfortunately, because the command-and-control model is the management style many in this cohort experienced as employees, their default setting remains a hierarchical management style. Many Boomers modeled their management style on those above them on the organizational ladder as a way of ensuring promotions and recognition. Today, they face the challenge of dealing with employees who demand a more collaborative management style and won't accept a directive top-down approach. However, many managers haven't been trained or coached on how to be more collaborative.

More and more Gen Xers have assumed positions of greater management responsibility. As employees, this cohort has desired a management style that is transparent and genuine. Many Gen Xers are skeptical that their manager has their best interests at heart, particularly competitive, politically focused Baby Boomer bosses. They want managers that will help grow their careers and improve their skill sets. Like Baby Boomers, Gen Xers are accustomed to managing others in the manner in which they have been managed—a diluted version of the command-and-control model. However, this generation demonstrates its own unique characteristics, with a management style that is characterized as straightforward. Because they are focused on results rather than relationships, Gen Xers sometimes forget the emotional element involved in managing. Their feedback tends to be direct and focused on the task at hand. It's business, not personal.

As managers, Gen Xers tend to be brutally honest with their direct reports on performance expectations and during performance reviews. Focused on achieving results means adopting a management style that motivates teams to reach high levels of performance on a consistent basis. While Gen X managers take a collaborative approach with their teams, they differentiate themselves from Baby Boomers in the type of collaboration they seek. While Boomers build consensus, Gen X managers understand their accountabilities as leaders and build teams based on individual competence and shared accountability, not mutual agreement.

Gen Ys are just beginning to enter into management roles as supervisors and team leads. They have yet to formalize their approach to managing others. However, based on what we know of this cohort's desire to be managed in a high-touch, personalized way, we can expect that Gen Ys will try to be inclusive managers. They will echo the boomer's desire for consensus while blending the Gen Xer's drive for results. This generation will no doubt maximize technology as a way of delivering personalized feedback to direct reports in a real-time, on-demand way.

Generational Clash Points

Lawrence has recently been promoted to a senior management position. As a Gen Xer, he has often encountered managers whom he didn't think were very effective. Sometimes, they would bark orders at him or, worse yet, yell. They rarely shared information with him about the big picture, strategy or direction of the team/department/organization; information was only parceled off on a need-to-know basis. He believes that his manager behaved that way so that he would remain the expert and Lawrence wouldn't supersede him. Lawrence wants to be a more collaborative and open manager with his team, but he is already facing some challenges. His direct reports are Gen Ys and haven't had a lot of work experience. He struggles with their expectation that he must provide them with a lot of direction and coaching to complete even simple tasks. This frustrates him as he is eager to achieve results. He is amazed at how dependant his team is on him to solve problems and give direction. He doesn't think his Gen Y employees are very independent. When Lawrence does provide feedback, it is often focused on areas of improvement rather than areas of strengths. He wants his team to understand what they need to do to get better. This has resulted in some Gen Y employees feeling like he is harsh and cold. In one instance, Lawrence gave feedback to a young employee that he felt was very balanced and fair. The result was the employee left the room crying. He's not sure what he needs to do, but he knows that his approach right now isn't working. He's a little worried about his reputation with senior leaders as they are evaluating his success as a new leader, but he's confident that he will be able to turn things around. He plans to talk to some friends this weekend to figure out how they have handled similar situations.

Section II

How to Get 'Em

Being an organization that invests in getting, keeping, and growing the best employees is a strategic business decision to improve your organizational performance. Human capital-focused organizations are characterized by their efforts to attract, retain, and develop competent and committed employees.[1] The best performing organizations devote time, attention, and resources to recruiting the right people the first time as this is the first step in building a talented, engaged, high-performance workforce. Also, the recruitment process is the first step in building engagement with employees. During the recruitment and orientation stages, candidates evaluate the transparency of your hiring process, your responsiveness at an individual level, and your ability to partner with them to create a win-win employment contract. They make judgments about your organization based on the way they are treated in the recruitment process. The appearance of incompetence, lack of respect, delays in the process, or a sense of being interrogated rather than courted can turn off potential new hires, especially those that have other employment options.[2]

In this chapter, we will explore how to *get* employees through recruitment and orientation and the role these stages play in establishing engagement with employees.

The Impact of an Effective Recruitment and Orientation Strategy

Creating an effective recruitment strategy is not a stand-alone process. You should consider the impact, both positive and negative, that your approach has on the rest of your people strategies. Getting the recruitment process right is often seen as a silver bullet in solving other organizational challenges such as turnover and poor performance. It's assumed that if your organization recruits better people, meaning identifying future stars quicker, then the other stages of the employee life cycle will run more smoothly. To some considerable extent, this is true. Eighty percent of turnover is the result of mistakes made during the recruitment process.[3] Energy and effort spent recruiting the right employees minimizes the work required to retain those employees and makes it easier to manage talent within your organization.

While recruitment identification is critical, so is the orientation process. An effective orientation program should focus on creating an *experience* for new employees that integrates them into their new work environment. The experience should be fun, informative, and motivating. The role of the organization and, most importantly, the manager during the orientation phase is to act as a gracious host. A poorly designed orientation program is like attending a poorly organized social event.

> You are invited to a party where everyone knows each other—except
> you. No one greets you when you arrive, there is no one to show you
> around and make introductions—you are left to fend for yourself.
> Compare that experience to being warmly greeted, introduced to
> the other guests and generally welcomed into the group.[4]

Employee orientation is the linchpin that binds your recruitment and retention strategies together. Without an effective orientation process, your efforts in the front end to bring top talent into the organization and in the back end to keep them will be jeopardized.

Chapter Three

Recruitment: Gaining Competitive Advantage

Many organizations can no longer rely on their products and services, processes, or access to consumer markets to achieve success; their competitive advantage is now dependent on selecting and managing a quality workforce.[1] Employees' abilities to obtain, create, manage, and transfer knowledge are critical in outperforming your competition. As a result, this requires that you recruit, retain, and develop high-performance employees.

Given the positive impact high-performance employees can have on your corporate performance, it's no wonder that leading organizations are focused on getting the best and the brightest. Regardless of whether you are recruiting knowledge workers, skilled workers, or laborers, finding employees who not only have the right skills and competencies but also the right attitude is essential to your organization's ability to succeed. The challenge is to determine how you can best recruit desirable employees when you are faced with a seller—or employee-driven market.

In our work with clients, we focus on the five components that are essential to creating a best practice recruitment strategy. They are the following:

1. Use a blended approach
2. Focus on cultural fit
3. Close the gap
4. Leverage your brand
5. Maximize internal recruiting strategies

Component 1: Use a Blended Approach

Before you can recruit employees, you must first ask yourself what skills, knowledge, and attitudes they should possess in order to contribute to your organization, department, or team success. This answer is your guide in determining *where and how* you can proactively source and recruit the right talent. A blended approach to recruitment requires that you reach out to potential candidates in a variety of ways. Incorporating the following recruitment activities into your recruitment strategy enhances your ability to tap into a diverse pool of potential candidates:

- online job posting
- recruitment fairs—on and off campus
- head hunters / recruitment agencies
- promoting your reputation as an employer of choice
- community involvement
- blogs developing internal talent

While each of the above recruitment activities is effective, they are most powerful when combined to create a customized approach to the target market. Most notably, online job postings allow your organizations to connect with large numbers of candidates on a global basis and facilitate a connection more quickly. The traffic volume of online job-search sites like Monster.com, HotJobs, and Workopolis is unprecedented. Jeff Taylor, who launched the world's largest job-search site, Monster.com, believes the main contribution his site has made to the recruitment process is to speed up the hiring process and increase the accuracy of the job-search process. He boasts, "You can post a job at 2:00 p.m. and get your first response at 2:01."[2] Candidates can review the posting, connect to your corporate website, or read your annual general report. However, online job postings are less effective when attempting to recruit highly knowledgeable or skilled employees. While online recruitment provides volume, it doesn't always guarantee quality. In this case, internal referrals or head hunters (recruiters) may prove to be a better approach.

Given the wide access to information provided through the Internet, online job seekers can now connect with other users to ask questions about what it's like to work for your company. They can also solicit opinions about your organization through blogs and chat groups. Online word of mouth or viral marketing has become an official vehicle in the recruitment process. If your employees, past and present, post positive messages about your organization and their experiences with managers, job seekers are likely to be influenced to consider you as a potential employer.

Southwest Airline[3]

> Southwest Airlines has just launched a corporate blog, http://*www.blogsouthwest.com*, where Southwest employees from all levels within the organization can post messages. The blog, which is branded "Nuts about Southwest" doubles as a communication vehicle for employees and an online marketing tool to promote the airline and its positive brand image.

On the flip side, we know that bad messages travel more quickly and are communicated in a louder voice than positive ones. If posted replies on external sites are negative, your organization may have trouble recruiting candidates. The impact of your organization's reputation and brand image on recruiting top talent is explored further in the fourth component—*leveraging your brand*.

When working with clients to create a blended approach to recruitment, we recommend incorporating a variety of tools and methods during the selection process. This ensures that you are achieving the highest level of validity. Assuming you have been able to attract several candidates through effective recruitment methods, you need to assess their individual abilities to meet the role requirements and fit within your corporate culture.

When evaluating which tools/methods to use during the selection process, there are a variety of factors to consider, including the cost to purchase or develop a tool as well as administrative costs. Another important consideration is how valid the tool is at predicting job performance. According to an analysis of several measurement tools/methods used by HR professionals, the most reliable and valid options are the following:[4]

Work samples	measures job skills though performance of tasks that are similar to those performed on the job.
Cognitive ability tests	measures mental abilities such as logic, reading comprehension, verbal or mathematical reasoning, and perceptual abilities.
Structured interviews	measures a variety of skills and abilities, particularly noncognitive skills such interpersonal skills and leadership style.

The best results are achieved through using a combination of selection tools to evaluate a candidate. Combining an ability test with a structured interview yields greater results and can provide richer data from which to compare candidates.

Wal-Mart[5]

Wal-Mart has recognized that relying exclusively on one method for evaluating candidates does not yield the best results. They have incorporated a blended approach to recruitment by training HR teams on a variety of selection and interviewing techniques. They also perform background checks for those who have reached the final stages of the hiring process.

A blended approach to recruitment also requires a focus on establishing ongoing relationships with potential candidates. Stay in touch even if positions aren't available right away or candidates aren't interested in working for your organization at this point in time. This tactic ensures that you have a continuous supply of candidates that meet your desired criteria when you do need to draw on them. Also, by acknowledging the impact spouses, partners, and parents play in the decision to accept employment, some organizations build a strong relationship with the influencers who have an impact on a candidate's decision-making process.

By taking a blended approach to your recruitment and selection process, you can attract and recruit more qualified, high-performance candidates than simply relying on a singular method, tool, or approach. In fact, there is evidence that organizations that use a blended approach to recruitment have higher levels of annual profit, profit growth, sales growth, and overall performance.[6]

Component 2: Focus on Cultural Fit

The most important attraction factor for candidates to an organization is the person-organization fit, satisfying the desire to feel like part of a group and share the same values and goals.[7] All too frequently, employees leave an organization not because they can't meet the requirements of their role, but because they don't fit within the culture.[8] The best way to avoid this outcome is to hire for attitude and cultural fit and then train for skills. It's much easier to develop skills and competencies than to modify employees' personalities, attitudes, or mindsets. Some organizations have gone so far as to identify the DNA of an ideal employee, which is used during the recruitment process to evaluate candidates.

Pfizer[9]

Pfizer, a world leader in the pharmaceutical industry, has identified six leader behaviors they expect from their employees. In the career section of their Web site, Pfizer states, "Leadership is not an end state at which one arrives—either as an individual or as a company. It must be earned every day. It must become an ongoing way of thinking, behaving, and performing, regardless of level or position. At Pfizer, it is a mandate for the many, not a select few." Their six leader behaviors serve as a guide for personal action.

Sustain Focus on Performance
Leaders sustain a focus on performance by setting the right priorities, adhering to high standards, being strategically opportunistic, and focusing on their customers.

Create an Inclusive Environment
Leaders create an inclusive environment by being open to new ideas, seeking always to include colleagues, and ensuring that all managers do the same.

Encourage Open Discussion and Debate
Leaders listen actively, encourage contribution, accept criticism, skillfully manage meetings, and discussions and communicate effectively.

Manage Change
Leaders manage change by anticipating strategically, taking initiative, and planning for better ways to operate. They empower people to act, train change agents, and seek better priorities.

Develop People
Leaders develop people in many ways. They practice helpful feedback, listen skillfully, plan for development, and serve as coach and mentor.

Align Across Pfizer
Leaders contribute to helping the company as a whole, communicate and collaborate with other Pfizer groups, and utilize and support our governance system.

You can create a culture-based recruitment process by considering not just the skills and knowledge required to perform a role, but also the cultural context in which the job is performed. Understanding the personality traits of those who excel at the role provides you with insights into the type of employee who will fit best within your culture. You can then evaluate candidates by including questions during the structured interview that uncover personality traits and attitudes.

In addition, a culture-based recruitment process requires continuously communicating your corporate values and highlighting the employee traits that you are seeking. Consistency in your messages is important as different levels of your organization may communicate different things externally to candidates. How your CEO describes your corporate culture shouldn't be drastically different from your line managers and employees. This consistency in messaging is critical in closing the gap between recruitment messages and actual workplace culture. In chapter 6, we will discuss in greater detail the connection between organizational values and communication.

Component 3: Close the Gap

It's natural for HR leaders, recruiters, and managers to want to present their organizations in the best possible light throughout the recruitment process. However, there is a serious risk when organizations overstate the positive attributes of their culture while not painting a realistic picture of their workplace. We caution our clients that if new employees expect their organization to behave in a particular way (e.g., collaborative team environment) based on the recruitment messages when, in fact, their culture is very different (e.g., hierarchical and bureaucratic), then employees will be more likely to disengage/disconnect.

Wal-Mart[10]

Wal-Mart found that there was a gap in the information being provided to candidates during the recruitment process and the actual job requirements. As a result, turnover increased. Their internal data revealed that associates left the organization within the first ninety days of employment because there was a conflict in their schedule, or they preferred to work in another area of the business. These issues were not being discussed during the hiring process, and therefore, employees were being hired without having a clear understanding of the employment expectations.

Research suggests that organizations only reveal the most positive information in their recruitment materials. Also, during interviews, managers communicate positive, rather than accurate, information about their workplace culture and job attributes.[11] The most effective way to close this gap is to provide candidates with a realistic picture of the job and your organization. Provide clear, specific, and complete information in recruitment materials so as to limit misinterpretations about the nature of the job or of your organizational culture. Be as transparent about your culture as possible. Equip managers with the skills and tools to conduct hiring conversations that are open and honest. It is critical that whatever is communicated and promised during the recruitment phase can and will be delivered once the new employee comes on board.

Ontario Power Generation[12]

A large public power utility, Ontario Power Generation, has developed a Web site for potential candidates (http://www.mypowercareer.com) that provides a realistic job preview (RJP) for key positions. The RJP provides an honest description of the rewards and challenges of the role. The objective is to achieve the right fit between job seekers and the job profile as well as help candidates form an accurate expectation of the job. By being transparent about the nature of the role and the organizational culture, Ontario Power Generation believes this will ultimately improve the working relationship with the employee. A RJP profile includes role-specific information about:

♦ the hiring process;
♦ life as a new—(tailored to each specific role);
♦ overview of the job (tailored to each specific role);
♦ training requirements and career opportunities;
♦ pay, benefits, and rewards;
♦ supervision;
♦ working conditions;
♦ rewards and challenges (tailored to each specific role);
♦ critical success factors;
♦ contact information.

If you are in the process of changing your corporate culture, you may tend to overrepresent desired cultural traits. The goal is to attract employees whose values, attitudes, and behaviors are aligned with the desired new direction of your organization. If you take this approach, we recommend that you share the fact that you are undergoing a culture shift with candidates. This way, they're aware of the role they will play in championing change and the potential cultural obstacles they will face.

Component 4: Leverage your Brand

One of the key contributors in recruiting top talent is an organization's reputation and brand. In short, reputation impacts recruitment outcomes. Organizations that have strong reputations are more highly desired by job seekers and influence candidates to positively perceive the benefits of working for them. This means that if you have a strong reputation and brand, there is pride associated in working for your organization. As a result, prospective candidates will actively seek employment with your organization and may even willingly accept a lower salary to become part of your team. On average, candidates are "willing to accept roughly 7 percent less salary to take an identical job at a firm with a positive reputation than a firm with a negative reputation."[13] This data also proves a positive correlation between your brand image/reputation and the bottom line costs of recruiting talent. If you have a strong organizational reputation, you may be able to recruit higher-quality employees while compensating the same or less than your competitors.

As we discussed earlier, the ability of job seekers to access unofficial information about your organization through online job-search sites, blogs, and newsgroups impacts their perceptions of your brand and organizational reputation. A negative perception of your organization/brand impacts the success of your recruitment efforts.

International Hotel Chain

A large international hotel chain with which we worked, faces the challenge of being blacklisted by students at a particular college campus. The students' attitudes are the result of a negative experience a small number of students had while participating in a summer internship program at the organization. Once the students returned to campus, the bad news story spread quickly. The organization's campus recruiters have had difficulty hiring from that campus for several years now since many students now hold a negative perception of the organization's reputation and management style.

A key factor in building a strong organizational reputation is your corporate social performance (CSP). Your CSP provides potential candidates with signals about your organizational values, corporate culture, and management practices. Similar to your consumer brand reputation, the greater your corporate social performance, the more attractive your organization is to top talent. If you have a strong CSP, leverage it as part of your recruitment efforts. Communicate to potential candidates the ways in which your organization makes a contribution.

Shell Canada[14]

As part of their communication to potential candidates, Shell Canada's Web site provides in-depth information about the organization's business principles. They believe that upholding the Shell reputation is paramount. "We are judged by how we act. Shell Canada's reputation will be upheld if we act with honesty and integrity in all our dealings, and we do what we believe to be right at all times within the legitimate role of business." The organization outlines their commitment to employees by stating, "Our actions are governed by our values and principles, our focus on corporate governance and by our commitment to sustainable development. We strive to treat people with respect and to operate with health and safety as workplace priorities." They go on to promote their CSP in the areas of respect and safeguard of people and working with Aboriginal communities.

Your ability to actively promote your organization's reputation, brand, and corporate social performance throughout the recruitment process increases the success rate of recruiting top talent. A full discussion of leveraging your brand through the communication and execution of an employee brand promise can be found in chapter 6.

Component 5: Maximize Internal Recruitment Strategies

Of all the methods available to recruit new talent, probably one of the strongest strategies is to tap into the talent that already exists within an organization. Developing internal talent is a particularly effective way of building bench strength that can be deployed across an organization when required. Internal development is a particularly good recruitment strategy when you are facing a tight labor market and short supply of knowledge, skilled, or labor workers. It reduces hiring costs by avoiding bidding wars for top talent and limits the number of positions that need to be filled by external people. Fewer resources are required to advertise jobs, post online, interview, administer and tabulate cognitive tests, as well as conduct reference checks. Another great advantage of developing talent from within is the confidence it inspires within employees. They recognize that they can grow, develop, and build their careers with your organization. The by-product for your organization is increased retention and engagement.

When you do need to source talent from outside of the organization, you can still draw on internal resources to help. Employee referral programs are particularly effective in attracting a pool of qualified talent. Some organizations offer a referral fee to existing employees—on average ranging from $100 to $2,000, but going as high as $6,000 for elite knowledge workers—if a candidate they recommend is hired by the organization. Given the high costs of recruiting "hot" skills, leveraging employee referrals creates a win-win-win for the organization, the employee, and the candidate. Since candidates' resumes are pushed to the top of the pile, the process is quicker and more responsive to them. For the employee, they are rewarded with a cash bonus and the knowledge that they have helped out a friend or family member. The organization wins by reducing recruiting costs, filling positions quicker, and gaining new hires who fit with the culture. Candidates that are referred by existing employees are less likely to turnover and more likely to be better performers.[15] This may be due to the fact that internal employees have a good understanding of the existing corporate culture and will refer candidates who would be a good fit with the organization/department/team.

Sierra Wireless[16]

Sierra Wireless places strong emphasis on their employee referral program (ERP) as a way of attracting high-quality candidates, speeding up the recruitment process, and rewarding existing employees. Their ERP rewards employees with $3,000 for each referral that is hired. The program is a success because employees feel empowered to make a contribution by referring candidates who will be good employees and will add value to the organization.

Demonstrating Organizational Engagement

To align with our characteristics of organizational engagement, your recruitment process should demonstrate transparency, responsiveness, and partnering.

To be transparent during recruitment, we recommend you inform candidates of all stages of your selection process, specifically how and why certain tools/methods are used to evaluate them. Be as open and honest about your corporate culture and describe types of employees who succeed in your organization. What common traits, attitudes, and skills do they possess? This allows candidates to self-identify whether or not they are a good fit with your organization. Be transparent about the role that candidates are applying for. By creating realistic job profiles, you are able to accurately communicate the positive and negative aspects of the role.

To demonstrate responsiveness, candidates should be informed of their results (i.e., test scores) and hiring decisions in a timely manner. Within legal parameters, as much justification as possible should be provided as to why a candidate has or has not been selected for employment.[17] Attempt to respond to candidates' questions and concerns in a timely manner, perhaps via online chat or a Q&A hotline. Also, minimize wait times between the steps in your recruitment process. This demonstrates to candidates your eagerness to reach an outcome.

To demonstrate partnering, candidates should be allowed to participate in a face-to-face interaction designed for two-way communication. Candidates should be encouraged to freely ask questions. Also, it's important for recruiters and managers to treat candidates as potential investors in your organization. What will their return on investment be? Seek to understand what's important to candidates as it relates to your corporate culture, work environment, management practices, and career opportunities. Partner with them to overcome obstacles that may prevent them from accepting employment with your organization. Also, partner with internal colleagues to ensure that your organization delivers consistent recruitment experiences that motivate and encourage candidates to join.

Generational Considerations

Each generation is motivated by different employment needs and expectations. What a Traditionalist is looking for in a positive employment relationship may be drastically different from what a Gen Xer wants or will accept. A one-size-fits-all approach to recruiting new employees ignores the unique requirements of each generational cohort. Since the objective is to create a win-win employment relationship, your recruitment approach should be customized to address generational expectations.

The more you can tap into the motivations of each generation, the more successful you will be at creating targeted recruitment strategies that align with generational expectations. For example, by incorporating key messages that resonate with each generation into a job posting, you will be more successful in attracting a pool of multigenerational candidates than using a generic approach. Highlighting the history and legacy of your organization speaks to Traditionalists' desires for a stable and strong organization where they can build a legacy. Emphasizing your organization's wellness programs and sabbaticals appeals to Baby Boomers who are seeking an opportunity for new career opportunities while managing high levels of stress. Communicating your organization's commitment to work-life balance appeals to the independent nature of Gen Xers. Gen Y candidates are most drawn to your organization's use of cutting-edge technology and your corporate social performance.

More and more, organizations are focusing on recruiting older workers given their availability, experience, and dedication. While many Traditionalists are already retired and Baby Boomers are beginning to leave the workforce, experienced workers (fifty-five years and above) will continue to be actively recruited in a hot job market to fill key positions. The best way to tap into this market is to position your organization as a desirable place to work for experienced workers. This means focusing on employment opportunities that allow for flexibility (part-time or contractual employment) so as to provide Traditionalists and older Baby Boomers with the opportunity to work a few hours a week as it fits within their schedule.

Avis[18]

At Avis, an international car-rental company, they actively seek employees in the 60-69 age range to be shuttlers (those that transport customers to and from the Avis depot). By tapping into this market, they gain employees that have maturity, can build good rapport with customers, and cost the company less through lower insurance rates. By offering very flexible work hours, Avis is able to attract employees that can, or wish to, only work a few hours a week or prefer to relocate during the winter months. For these employees and Avis, their work arrangement is a win-win; the organization benefits by tapping into employees' wealth of experience and employees participate in a social work environment characterized by camaraderie and teamwork, while earning an income.

An area of emphasis when recruiting Baby Boomers should be how your organization exposes employees to new projects and involves them in activities that contribute to your market leadership. Involvement in new product launches and market share growth projects appeal to this cohort by reinforcing that they can be part of a winning team and make a contribution to the organization in a meaningful way. Opportunities to build their profile through corporate representation in associations and external committees appeals to Baby Boomers' need to identify themselves through their career.

Regardless of which methods or strategies you use in developing a blended approach to recruitment, it's important to recognize that all generations are interested in challenging work, a supportive manager, and a positive work environment. However, the younger generations are much more likely to want to peek behind the curtain during the recruitment process to ensure that you can deliver on the deal. They want to determine whether or not the recruitment promises you make are likely to come true. For example, candidates may request to speak to current employees to evaluate their prospective manager's reputation and to review policies and procedures related to work-life balance, sabbaticals, and performance management. As discussed in component 2—close the gap—there must be alignment between the messages communicated and opportunities proposed by your recruiters and your line managers. Otherwise, Gen X and Gen Y candidates will sense a disconnect and will question your organization's ability to deliver on the employment deal. Gen Xers and Gen Ys hold a manager accountable for the promises made during the recruitment process. We know that the grace period that Gen X and Gen Y employees give an organization that is not fulfilling its recruitment promises is much shorter than what Traditionalists and Baby Boomers accept. You will likely have only three to six months to get it right before there is an impact on retention and employee engagement.

Some managers and recruiters are shocked and taken aback by younger candidates' aggressiveness during the interview process. Some managers feel that when they're interviewing Gen X candidates that they are the ones on the hot seat. They feel that *they* (the managers) are being interviewed, not the other way around. For example, a manager at a global consumer products company was shocked when a Gen X candidate asked what his next assignment would be and when he could expect a career move. The Baby Boomer manager felt that this type of questioning was bold and inappropriate—the candidate had not even proven himself, and yet he already wanted to know his next career move. For the Gen X candidate, opportunities for career growth and the speed at which opportunities could happen were valid criteria in evaluating the job offer.

When recruiting Gen Ys, it's important to recognize that this cohort is likely to seek out the opinions of their parents and peers when making employment decisions. You can leverage these influencers by also targeting them in your recruitment efforts. Parents that think highly of your organization will encourage their children to work for you. Peers that have positive experiences with your organization are more likely to tell their friends and encourage them to work for you. Since Gen Ys tend to move in packs, this can have both a positive and negative impact on your recruitment efforts. If your organization is perceived to be a great place to work, Gen Y employees are likely to refer their friends through internal employee referral programs or apply for positions en mass. On the flip side, if your organization is viewed as not such a great place to work, Gen Ys will discourage their friends from joining the organization or, worse, will leave the organization en mass.

Designing an integrated recruitment strategy that speaks to all four generations involves more than just a commitment from the HR team. Senior management must acknowledge that a one-size-fits-all approach to recruitment is ineffective in tapping into different employee markets. Also, since most HR practices and processes are founded on Traditionalist and Baby Boomer values, it may be a challenge for recruiters and managers to adjust to the increasing demands and straightforward negotiation style of younger candidates. By understanding generational motivations and expectations, you can actively and successfully manage the recruitment and orientation process.

Metrics That Matter

Some examples of quantitative metrics you can use to evaluate your recruitment strategy are the following:

- Speed to hire—how rapid is the hiring process?
- Turnover of new recruits
- Number of internal promotions
- Number of key roles filled by internal versus external resources
- Number of employees who refer candidates
- Number of referrals that translate into job offers/hires
- Number of applications per job posting
- Reputation audit—how do target employee market(s) perceive your organization?
- Number of new hires from each generation

Sample Engagement Survey—Recruitment

Transparency demonstrated by specific, accurate, and open communication

- ☐ Do candidates know and understand all the steps in your recruitment process?
- ☐ Do candidates understand how the measurement tools/methods relate to the selection process?
- ☐ Are candidates provided with realistic and specific information about your workplace culture and job requirements?

Responsiveness demonstrated by timeliness and feedback

- ☐ Are candidates being processed quickly enough?
- ☐ Are hiring decisions provided to candidates in an informative and timely manner?
- ☐ Is feedback on the effectiveness of the recruitment process solicited from candidates?

Partnering demonstrated by the organization/managers collaborating with employees

- ☐ Are candidates able to access internal resources (HR, managers, team members) to ask questions?
- ☐ Is your recruitment strategy designed to achieve a win-win employment relationship?
- ☐ Does the recruitment process allow for non-punitive two-way communication?

* *While these questions are based on a yes/no response, a Likert scale may provide richer data, depending on the size and complexity of your organization. Be sure to analyze data along demographic lines as well.*

Chapter Four

Orientation: Sealing the Psychological Deal

Once you have recruited new employees, it's important that they experience some form of orientation that binds them to your organization, their manager, and their team. This may be accomplished through informal methods or more formal programs that include on-the-job training and extend over several months. Either way, the objective of an orientation program is to inculcate your corporate values, to have them build emotional and rational ties to your organization and the management team, and to bring them up to competency.

Assuming the role of a gracious host during the orientation stage ensures a positive and lasting impression of an organization. We ensure that our clients' orientation programs are a success by supporting new hires in the transition to their new role. We collaborate with HR to assist with this process by designing tools that help employees perform their role competently and consistently. The tools should support each stage of the transition, from their first day of work to their first anniversary. For example, providing new hires with interview questions they can ask key internal customer/colleagues helps them gain valuable insights into your organization and how they can add value.[1]

Also, a successful orientation program minimizes new employees' feelings of buyer's regret. This is your opportunity to seal the psychological deal by demonstrating how you will deliver on the promises that were made during the recruitment phase. The key messages and interactions employees experience during orientation should be consistent with what they experienced during the recruitment stage. Managers may have painted a rosy picture of their department during hiring interviews. But often, during the orientation stage, new employees are bombarded with war stories from colleagues about what it's really like to work at your organization. Ensure new employees are teamed up with a colleague who presents a positive yet accurate account of the role and how to succeed in your department/organization.

Wal-Mart[2]

Wal-Mart believes the future success of an employee's career is often imprinted in the first few months on the job. As a result, they focus on exposing new employees to the mainstream products/activities of the business and most importantly, to the leaders of the organization. It is mandated that managers participate in new employee orientation meetings so that the employee-manager relationship can be established from the outset. "The connection between those who work in the store, plant or department and those who make the decisions cannot be understated."

Whenever possible, senior leaders should be engaged in the orientation process, be it formal or informal, to set the big picture context of how the new hires' roles fit and contribute to organizational goals. Orientation is an ongoing process, not to be limited to just the first day or first week of new employment. Managers should touch base with new employees on a weekly basis for the first few months. Orientation efforts should also not be limited to just entry-level positions or one area of your business (e.g., sales). All employees, regardless of level, function, or age, should participate in an orientation process. The point is to reinforce to them that they have made the right employment decision and that they are being set up for success with your organization.

An effective approach to orientation, which is often overlooked, is reorientating existing employees. This involves developing a specific orientation program for long-standing employees with the objective of reengaging them and reorientating them to your organization's direction, objectives, and culture. When employees have worked at your organization for years, they may become disconnected from your organization's direction, particularly if you have undergone organizational changes. Reorienting employees to your organization creates a stronger, more cohesive cultural environment. It ensures greater clarity and consistency across the organization, which benefits the process of integrating new hires.

Some organizations recognize that younger employees in particular need additional support during the orientation stage in order to successfully integrate into their culture. As a result, our Navigating the Business Environment workshop is often incorporated as part of a larger orientation program. The emphasis is on helping new entrants to the workplace understand the existing corporate culture, including the generational values, expectations, and behaviors of managers and senior leaders. By revealing how others in the organization may perceive and/or misinterpret certain behaviors based on generational values (e.g., respect for authority or work style), new hires are set up for success. They learn tips and techniques on how to successfully collaborate with their manager and team to ensure a smooth integration into their new role. Managers are also coached on how to support new hires through the orientation process to strengthen the relationship and minimize feelings of buyer's regret.

Government Agencies

A number of government agencies and departments have asked for services for their "young professional networks". Recognizing that a large percentage of experienced government employees will be eligible for retirement in the next three to five years, senior leaders are actively supporting the creation and development of these networks. Often the focus of training sessions is on understanding generational differences as a way of empowering Gen Ys to recognize their ability to influence within work teams. They learn tips for career success and identify how to create a win-win relationship with their manager and colleagues within the first ninety days on the job. Given that government has a strong culture built on Traditionalist and Baby Boomer values, the younger generations often need tips and techniques on how to navigate their careers and make a difference within a public sector environment.

If you don't currently have a formal orientation program, we strongly suggest that you create one. Given the increasing demand for top talent and the need to retain employees as long as possible, you must work to seal the psychological deal in the first phase of employment. Failing to do so can result in disengaged employees, loss of productivity, and higher, costly turnover.

Demonstrating Organizational Engagement

For your orientation process to demonstrate the characteristics of organizational engagement, it needs to focus on engaging as many key people across your organization as possible. Revealing how each business contributes to overall corporate success allows new hires to see the big picture as it relates to their role and their future with the company. Transparency in your orientation program also means clearly stating objectives and outcomes. By communicating what you hope to achieve through your formal or informal orientation initiatives, both new hires and managers/leaders understand the expectations of the roles they play and their accountabilities. A responsive orientation process is fluid and flexible—adapting to business needs and employees' needs. It solicits feedback from new hires on the effectiveness of the orientation process, their perceptions of the organization, and any additional managerial support required to succeed in their new role. By doing so, you are also demonstrating partnering by supporting new hires in their transition and working with them to ensure they are set up for success. A robust orientation program that demonstrates organizational engagement helps to seal the psychological deal and engage new employees.

Generational Considerations

Once you have selected and hired new employees, your orientation process should be aligned to generational expectations. Your Traditionalist and Baby Boomer new hires want an orientation process that establishes their rank and order within the organization. By providing these cohorts with a landscape of the key players, they have a sense of where within the organization they can/should network and build partnerships. Traditionalists appreciate learning about your company's history, reputation, and contribution to the community. Baby Boomers are eager to meet senior people so that they can begin to establish strategic relationships, making themselves known in the organization. Reorientation programs can also serve as a way of reconnecting with disengaged Traditionalists and Baby Boomers—in particular, those who may not feel as tied to your organization as they once did or those who don't understand new organizational changes.

To strengthen Gen Xers' ties to the organization, we recommend that you ensure new recruits meet and form relationships with a variety of managers/senior leaders during the orientation process. Given that this generation is loyal to their manager, the greater the depth and breath of their roots within your organization, the less likely they are to leave. It's during the orientation process that you build the foundation for strong retention of Gen X employees. Gen X and Gen Y employees expect to be introduced to senior leaders and to have full disclosure regarding their role, their level of decision making, and their expected performance outcomes. Gen Ys in particular should be briefed on the level of managerial support they can expect to receive and the frequency of coaching sessions. This cohort is highly engaged in orientation programs that establish a sense of camaraderie because this group forms networks and relationships with their peers, across departments. Also, Gen Ys are motivated by orientation programs that allow them to be exposed to different parts of your business. Setting Gen Ys up for success by providing them with the tools necessary to navigate your business environment builds trust and confidence that you are committed to their career growth and long-term success within your organization.

Metrics That Matter

Some examples of quantitative metrics you can use to evaluate your orientation strategy are the following:

- Management involvement in the orientation process
- New recruits' feedback on the process
- New recruits' knowledge of corporate values, processes, and practices
- Integration of new recruits into the workplace culture at a departmental and team level

Sample Engagement Survey—Orientation

Transparency demonstrated by specific, accurate, and open communication

- ☐ Are the messages communicated during the recruitment process and orientation process consistent?

- ☐ Are new employees provided with the information and tools required to be effective in their roles?

- ☐ Are new employees informed of the organizational/departmental/team/individual performance goals in the first month?

Responsiveness demonstrated by timeliness and feedback

- ☐ Do managers connect with new recruits on an on-going basis within the first three months?

- ☐ Are feelings of buyer's regret discussed and overcome?

- ☐ Is feedback on the effectiveness of your orientation process solicited from new hires?

Partnering demonstrated by the organization/managers collaborating with employees

- ☐ Are new hires exposed to a range of managers and senior leaders?
- ☐ Are new hires formally welcomed into the organization and team?
- ☐ Are new hires partnered with colleagues to help with the transition?

* *While these questions are based on a yes/no response, a Likert scale may provide richer data, depending on the size and complexity of your organization. Be sure to analyze data along demographic lines as well.*

Section III

How to Keep 'Em

You have recruited the right person for the right job, at the right time. You have created orientation programs, both formal and informal, designed to seal the psychological deal. Now, you have the challenge of ensuring that employees stay with your organization as long as possible—building long-term commitment. As we discussed in chapter 1, employment relationships are open-ended. Employees are investors who expect an increasing return on their investment. Just as financial investors review quarterly statements to analyze their rate of return, employees review their investment with your organization continuously. They are evaluating whether or not they are giving more than they are getting. This chapter discusses the types of strategies and mechanisms your organization needs to implement in order to build a culture of retention—a culture in which employees can easily evaluate their ROI. And a culture that encourages employees to renegotiate with you first before leaving to negotiate a better deal with your competitor.

Prior to the employment deal being broken in the mid-'80s, organizations didn't concern themselves a lot with the issue of retention. Employees joined organizations with the mindset that they would work there for years, decades, or even their whole career. Organizations counted on this long-term commitment mindset, defined it, and called it loyalty. During the mass downsizing era, organizations broke the employment deal by no longer rewarding loyalty with job security. This event sparked a transition period, where the employee mindset began to shift. Employees realized that they couldn't rely on their employers to take care of them; they were in charge of managing their own careers. Commitment shifted to developing and maintaining professional skill sets rather than being loyal to an employer. However, in many cases, organizations were unaware of this slow shift in employee thinking because there were still more employees than jobs. There was no need to focus on what employees wanted because organizations and managers were in control of the employment relationship.

The abundance of supply started to dwindle in the late '90s. First, within the IT sector, as Y2K, enterprise-wide software, and the World Wide Web gained a foothold. During the high-tech/IT boom, we started to see what a demand-side labor market looked like. Not only was it hard for organizations to recruit employees, but it also became increasingly difficult to keep good people. An organization's brand or reputation held less and less weight. Even large well-established multinational companies struggled to attract and retain top talent. Traditionally, organizations in the brick-and-mortar world were prize employers highly sought after by new graduates and experienced employees. However, quickly, the "click-and-mortar" world of IT and high tech looked a lot more attractive to employees. It offered exciting work that was shaping the future and was high paying and provided a work culture that was less stuffy and more flexible than traditional organizations. During this time, organizations began to analyze the challenge of retention in a more meaningful way. Initially, they believed that by paying more, people would stay. However, it became clear that more compensation wasn't the silver bullet to solve retention challenges. As a result, retention strategies and mechanisms were broadened to include non-financial solutions.

Now, we realize that retention is both the responsibility of the organization as a strategic initiative and the responsibility of managers through the execution of those strategies. In this section, we will discuss two people strategies that allow you to keep employees: total rewards, with a focus on recognition programs, and employee brand promises.

Chapter Five

Total Rewards Programs: What's My ROI?

Money isn't everything. Employees leave your organization for non-financial reasons such as lack of challenging assignments or poor relationships with their managers.[1] We have heard countless stories of senior managers throwing money at an employee who is at high risk of leaving their organization, only to be rewarded by a resignation letter a few months later. Pay definitely isn't the answer in a demand-side labor market. There is only so much money that you can offer to internal and external employees before you drive yourself out of the market. If high pay is the only reason that new employees come to your organization and existing ones stay, then each group is at a high risk of turnover. All it will take is for another organization to offer more money.[2] As an owner of a trucking company once asked us, "What should we do, when for 50 cents more an hour drivers will cross the street to our competition?" Sadly, many organizations haven't realized that total rewards programs need to be comprehensive to retain employees. A European study completed by 367 companies, in nineteen countries, across fourteen industries showed that 50 percent of companies didn't include more than compensation and benefits within their total rewards description.[3]

Sample Total Rewards Programs

Check out the following Web sites of organizations that advertise their total rewards
programs:

American Century Investments
http://*www.americancenturey.com*

Tektronix
http://*www.tek.com*

TSX Group
http://*www.tsx.com*

Roche
http://*www.roche.com*

Astrazeneca
(Canada and United States—different programs)
http://*www.astrazeneca.ca* or http://*www.astrazeneca.com*

The objective behind a total rewards program is to create an environment that
makes your organization the all-around most attractive place to stay and build a
career. Your organization should communicate all of the benefits of working for
your organization. Employees need to recognize that the payback of working at your
organization includes more than just compensation and benefits. In its most robust
form, total rewards include both financial (tangible) and non-financial (intangible)
benefits. The diagram below illustrates many of the components that comprise a
total rewards program.

Total Rewards Programs

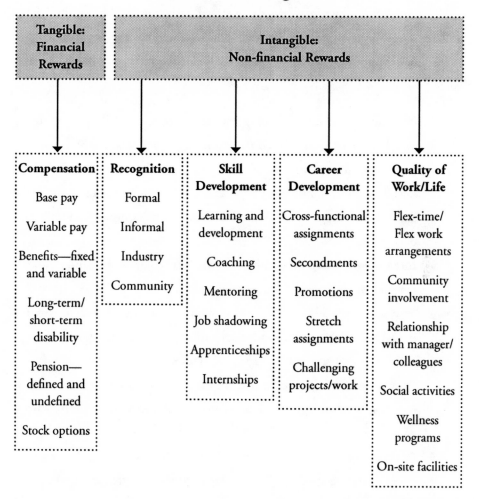

Tangible: Financial Rewards	Intangible: Non-financial Rewards			
Compensation	**Recognition**	**Skill Development**	**Career Development**	**Quality of Work/Life**
Base pay	Formal	Learning and development	Cross-functional assignments	Flex-time/ Flex work arrangements
Variable pay	Informal	Coaching	Secondments	Community involvement
Benefits—fixed and variable	Industry	Mentoring	Promotions	
Long-term/ short-term disability	Community	Job shadowing	Stretch assignments	Relationship with manager/ colleagues
Pension— defined and undefined		Apprenticeships	Challenging projects/work	Social activities
Stock options		Internships		Wellness programs
				On-site facilities

Financial rewards include any pay or service that has a fixed dollar amount attached to it. Besides salary and bonus, these rewards include health care and disability and other benefit packages. Non-financial rewards are components that are indirectly quantifiable or not quantifiable at all. However, these components have perceived value to employees. For example, a recognition token has a dollar value, but the actual value may be far greater because the recipient perceives the value of the recognition to be significant. This concept of real value versus perceived value is particularly true of components under skill development, career development, and quality of work-life. For components that are difficult to quantify such as relationships, community involvement, or stretch assignments, the perceived value of these components remains an essential value in a total rewards program.

In building a total rewards program, the following principles should act as a guide:[4]

- **Holistic**: Focus on how employers recruit, retain, and motivate employees to contribute to organizational success using an array of financial and non-financial rewards.

- **Best fit**: Adopt a contingency approach—total rewards programs need to be tailored to the organization's culture, structure, work process, and business objectives.

- **Integrative**: Deliver innovative rewards that integrate with other human resource management policies and practices.

- **Strategic**: Align all aspects of reward to business strategy—total rewards are driven by business needs and reward business activities, employee behavior, and values that support strategic goals and objectives.

- **People-centered**: Recognize that employees are a key source of sustainable competitive advantage and focus on what employees value in the total work environment.

- **Customized**: Identify a flexible mix of rewards that offers choice and is designed to meet employees' needs, expectations, lifestyles, and stages of life.

- **Distinctive**: Use a complex and diverse set of rewards to create a powerful and unique brand that serves to differentiate organization from competitors.

- **Evolutionary**: Recognize that a total rewards approach is a long-term process based on incremental, rather than radical, changes.

- **Communicated**: Plan and schedule regular message delivery by the manager and the organization.

- **Executable**: Deliver consistently program components by the organization and managers.

Total rewards programs are not created overnight; they must strategically be aligned to your business objectives. A total rewards program isn't a bundle of perks for employees; rather, it is a strategic program designed to ensure maximum performance of your workforce. If your total rewards program can tap into the motivations and expectations of your workforce, then employees will demonstrate increased levels of engagement by expending discretionary effort, being more emotionally connected to your organization, and accepting accountability. In the area of quality of work-life, you have the greatest ability to impact employee engagement levels. Since the value of non-financial components may not always be obvious, it is in these areas that you can greatly impact employees' perceptions of value. We work with our clients to understand what their employees value, assessing whether or not their total rewards program truly taps into all employee groups, while making sure that it is aligned with the principles described above. The challenge is bringing to life each component of your total rewards program. This is the greatest obstacle to success. Having a total rewards program that successfully impacts retention rates means more than just packaging and branding existing or new programs; that's just the first step. The second step is consistent execution and communication of the components with ongoing evaluation and refinement. We evaluate how our clients can bring the execution and communication of their total rewards program to life at an organizational level and managerial level.

Demonstrating Organizational Engagement

As with any strategy or program, to increase employee engagement, your total rewards program must demonstrate the characteristics of organizational engagement—transparency, responsiveness, and partnering. The methods, vehicles, and processes at both an organizational and managerial level should demonstrate transparency in executing and communicating your total rewards program. Organizationally, human resource departments design and develop programs that create a framework for an attractive work environment. Through a variety of vehicles, like intranets, special events, and yearly reviews, you inform employees about how your total rewards program is being delivered to them. However, managers—from the executive team down to the supervisor level—need to play an active role in executing the program within the framework. Otherwise, you won't be successful in creating a culture of retention. By relying on the non-financial components of your total rewards program, you can motivate, develop, and effectively lead your teams and maximize your ability to keep 'em.

A total rewards program can be responsive if, in the construction phase, your organization first understands what is important to employees, both individually and collectively, before creating the best mix of financial and non-financial rewards. It's impossible, due to cost and operational limits, to give employees everything they want. So the key to success is to determine what is *most* meaningful to different employee groups, keeping in mind that generational identities have an impact on what each cohort perceives as valuable.

By managing expectations and offering opportunities to negotiate and select options within your total rewards program, you can partner with employees to create a win-win outcome. In addition, by having strong one-on-one relationships with employees, managers can demonstrate responsiveness and partnering by valuing each employee's desires. Essential to the relationship is understanding what makes the employment relationship a winning one for him/her.

Generational Considerations

The greater the flexibility and variety of your total rewards approach, the more likely it will be people-centered and the more likely it will address the values, expectations, and behaviors of all four generations. Each generational cohort, because of its unique identity, places higher levels of value on certain components within your total rewards program. The chart below highlights the key components which each cohort places greatest value on. Of course, this holds true only as long as base pay and benefits are within the acceptable range of industry and role standards.

Generational Emphasis within Total Rewards

Traditionalists	Promotions, incentives and stocks, health benefits (life/disability), pension, stability, formal recognition, community involvement
Boomers	Promotions, high-visibility projects, brand reputation, external company representation, support around work-life issues, personal learning and development, secondments, on-site facilities, industry recognition
Gen Xers	Training and development, challenging tasks/stretch assignments, independent work environment, project variety, work-life balance, two-way communication and coaching, flex work arrangements, variable pay
Gen Ys	Corporate citizenship, meaningfulness of work/products, manager feedback, casual work environment, work-life balance, access to senior leaders, mentoring, social activities, customer interaction, community involvement, flex-time

Each cohort is drawn to and emphasizes different components within a total rewards approach. So it's important that both the organization and managers recognize and emphasize the relevant components. It's also important that your organization communicates its commitment to each component of the program. When communicating, consistently reinforce how components are tied to achieving organizational objectives. For example, Baby Boomers, as the sandwich generation, may work for your organization because one of your key messages is a respect for work-life balance. However, if they don't feel supported by their managers in managing their time to meet family commitments, then their perception will be that this component of your total rewards program has no value to the organization. These Baby Boomers will not believe that they are getting a return on their investment. If the non-financial components of your total rewards program score poorly on a perceived value scale with each generational cohort, then you will be less likely to retain all four employee groups over the long term.

One of the reasons employees leave an organization is because of their relationship with their manager. This applies equally to all four generations; however, the younger generations are more apt to leave an organization more quickly than previous generations. Traditionalists and Baby Boomers often stay with an employer because they have an affiliation to the organization that overrides a dislike or disconnect with their immediate manager. These cohorts recognize that managers move on, leave or are terminated. They are more willing to accept that they will have good managers and bad managers throughout their careers. Gen X and Gen Y employees have very high expectations of their managers. We discussed in chapter 2 that the younger generations respect managers based on competence. Competence refers to functional and managerial proficiency. Gen Xers and Gen Ys expect managers to be great at: (a) providing feedback and helping them to improve (coaching), (b) tying the work that they do to business objectives and strategies (communication), and (c) building and managing effective teams (collaboration). From their perspective, managers who are good at all three of these skills—coaching, communication, and collaboration—are more likely to be able to develop their skills and help them realize their full potential. In the next section titled "How to Grow 'Em," we delve deeper into the management practices required to engage all four generations.

Recognition Programs

As one component of a total rewards program, we use recognition programs as an example to demonstrate how the execution of this component is strategically important. Just as we recommend taking a broad approach to a total rewards program, we suggest the same for formal recognition. If the only type of recognition your organization offers employees is based on years of service, then your ability to retain employees, particularly younger ones, is compromised. Today, most organizations recognize employees for more than just time served because they acknowledge that performance levels are equally, if not more, important. Also, organizations have come to realize that recognition doesn't have to be shown only through monetary tokens. Organizations have greater success with recognition programs when the tokens of recognition are tailored to what motivates and engages employees. By working with a wide range of organizations, we've noticed repetitive themes as to what makes employees feel recognized, both formally and informally.

There are three components to a successful recognition program: (1) the criteria for recognition, (2) the type of recognition offered, and (3) the participants involved in the process.

Recognition Criteria

- ✓ exceeding performance targets
- ✓ demonstrating organizational values in achieving targets
- ✓ years of service

Recognition Tokens

- ✓ money
- ✓ material items
- ✓ time off
- ✓ donations

Recognition Participation

- ✓ senior leaders—both internal to the organization and the parent company
- ✓ managers
- ✓ peers
- ✓ community/industry associations

Kraft Foods

Kraft Foods has a very robust rewards and recognition program that recognizes performance as well as the demonstration of Kraft Leadership behaviors. There are multiple levels of programs that can be initiated by associates, managers or senior leaders. In one example, Managers can recognize individual employees or teams other through the 'above and beyond the call of duty' (ABCD) award. The award recognizes individuals with both a monetary award as well as a token crystal memento. There is also the opportunity for associates to recognize each other or managers through the 'way to go' award. This program in general, encourages the recognition of positive contributions to the organization.

As with total rewards programs, a recognition program should contain a hybrid of all three recognition criteria to motivate and retain a multigenerational workforce. Only focusing on achieving performance targets may lead to a corporate culture where values and people are neglected in a drive to achieve results. The benefits of including the criteria of demonstrating corporate values is that organizations can change their culture over time by recognizing and rewarding different behaviors.

While the different types of recognition may seem difficult to quantify monetarily, in reality, each token can be translated into an equivalent dollar value. For example, time off, has a monetary value that can be prorated based on salary or hourly wage. What is more important, though, than the actual value of the recognition token is the perceived value of the token. For some employees, a couple of hours or a full day off work is perceived to have a greater value than money. Recognition participation should be as inclusive as possible—managers should be encouraged to recognize their direct reports, colleagues should recognize their colleagues, and direct reports should be able to recognize their manager. At the Bank of America, both managers and associates can present an associate with a Customer Experience Leadership Award plaque that recognizes exceptional performance.[5]

Demonstrating Organizational Engagement

Whatever criteria you use for your recognition programs, they should be openly known by all employees. Employees should know how the criteria will be measured and what behaviors they need to demonstrate to be considered for recognition. The employees selected for recognition should be celebrated publicly, and the reasons for their selection should be announced and publicized. Such a practice creates a transparent environment where other employees can follow in their colleagues' footsteps. An even more effective way to demonstrate organizational engagement would be to involve direct reports in recognizing managers. Recognition programs that allow for bottom-up recognition show high levels of responsiveness and partnering because they encourage two-way feedback. It's a strong strategy; managers who are recognized also serve as role models to other managers and, therefore, encourage an environment of high performance among managers. Also, a process that encourages bottom-up recognition demonstrates that the organization expects all employees—managers and individual contributors alike—to walk the talk. By customizing the tokens to what's important to your employees, you are partnering with them to ensure that they truly feel recognized. Offering a range of tokens that can be selected or knowing specifically what each employee values shows a high level of collaboration rather than an impersonal top-down management approach.

Generational Considerations

Just as generational identities influence the perceived value of each component of your total rewards, so will each generation place varying degrees of emphasis on the recognition tokens and the ability to participate in recognition programs. Traditionalists expect to be recognized for commitment and years of dedicated service. Many in this cohort place value on service pins, watches, and letters from the executive team congratulating and thanking them for their commitment and loyalty. Baby Boomers, because of their desire to add value and put their stamp on things, feel most recognized through promotions—a promotion means that the organization feels they are valuable to the team. However, public recognition like a departmental meeting announcement and material items (especially status items) also hold value with this cohort. Gen Xers are less driven by organizational recognition and place greater value in receiving time off. In addition, recognition for Gen Xers means being assigned to a new project or a new challenge where they can gain new marketable skills and achieve results. For Gen Ys, recognition in the form of time off would be at the top of their list. An even greater token would be if they received paid time off to volunteer at an organization of their choice.

Managers play a great role in the informal day-to-day recognition of team members. The key generational difference in informal recognition is that the younger generations emphasize frequency, whereas the older generations value the level of personal contact. Naturally, given the Gen Ys' identity, they appreciate informal feedback and recognition more frequently than other generations. For Gen Xers, they appreciate just-in-time manager feedback and recognition. For this generation, waiting until the departmental meeting each quarter to receive recognition verbally is not as valuable as a manager who sends an e-mail right away to acknowledge good work. When conducting focus groups on recognition at a financial institution, we learned that many Baby Boomers and Traditionalists feel that simple but personal gestures go the farthest. For example, a thank-you card, a thank-you e-mail with a senior manager copied, or stopping by to say thank-you were all significantly valued. Perhaps, one of the best approaches is being taken by Baptist Health Care in Florida, which surveyed its employees to understand what each employee values most. Employees ranked their preferences so that recognition could be personalized. Not only would this approach align perfectly with Gen Ys who want their tokens to be personalized, but it also demonstrates organizational engagement by being responsive to employee needs and partnering with them to better engage, motivate, and retain them.

Metrics That Matter

Some examples of quantitative metrics you can use to evaluate the success of your total rewards programs include the following:

- ✌ Turnover rate—voluntary/involuntary
- ✌ Departure reasons—exit interviews
- ✌ Retention rate within the first year
- ✌ Total rewards program effectiveness measured by employees' likelihood to stay with the organization—one, two, five years, etc.
- ✌ Total rewards program effectiveness measured by manager execution of components

Metrics That Matter

Some examples of quantitative metrics you can use to evaluate the success of your recognition program include the following:

- ✌ Types of tokens selected
- ✌ Recognition program participation (percentage)
- ✌ Management scores on engagement/satisfaction surveys pertaining to delivering formal and informal recognition

Sample Engagement Survey—Total Rewards Programs

Transparency demonstrated by specific, accurate, and open communication

☐ Does each employee receive a yearly calculation of their total rewards components?

☐ Is your total rewards program customized and the best fit for your organization's culture and objectives?

☐ Do you communicate in your recruitment and retention messages the uniqueness of your total rewards program?

Responsiveness demonstrated by timeliness and feedback

☐ Do you know what components of your total rewards program your employees value most?

☐ Do you ask employees what improvements should be made to your total rewards program so that you meet your strategic objectives?

☐ Has your total rewards program evolved over time?

Partnering demonstrated by the organization/managers collaborating with employees

☐ Can employees negotiate/renegotiate their total rewards programs?

☐ Are managers measured on their ability to execute on your total rewards programs?

☐ Do managers know which components of your total rewards program that employees value most?

*   *While these questions are based on a yes/no response, a Likert scale may provide richer data, depending on the size and complexity of your organization. Be sure to analyze data along demographic lines as well.*

Sample Engagement Survey—Recognition Programs

Each component of your total rewards program should be evaluated against the characteristics of organizational engagement.

Transparency demonstrated by specific, accurate, and open communication

- ☐ Do employees know the criteria and process of your recognition program?
- ☐ Do you regularly publicize the recipients of all rewards?
- ☐ Is your recognition program clearly linked to your business goals?

Responsiveness demonstrated by timeliness and feedback

- ☐ Do your managers provide informal recognition on a timely basis?
- ☐ Are employees involved in selecting the types of recognition tokens included in your program?
- ☐ Is it possible for various business units to customize the criteria of recognition, tokens, and participation to their operational reality?

Partnering demonstrated by the organization/managers collaborating with employees

- ☐ Can employees select their preferred type of recognition token?
- ☐ Can employees recognize managers and senior leaders?
- ☐ Do managers tailor their formal and informal recognition to individual employee desires?

* *While these questions are based on a yes/no response, a Likert scale may provide richer data, depending on the size and complexity of your organization. Be sure to analyze data along demographic lines as well.*

Chapter Six

Employee Brand Promises:
Say What You Mean and Do as You Say

The four generations, with their unique identities and behaviors, create a cultural dynamic in the workplace. Depending on the percentage of Traditionalists, Baby Boomers, Gen Xers, and Gen Ys, organizational cultures have informal and formal codes of conduct that are determined by the dominant group. Specifically, it is in the day-to-day management of teams that the codes of conduct determined by managers are most obvious. The everyday rules set by managers include the length of the workday; how, when, and where breaks are taken; meeting structures; project assignments; and the distribution of recognition, among many other things.

At an organizational level, formal codes of conduct are also created through the definition of values. Most organizations have a statement that defines the values that guide the behaviors of employees in the organization. Sometimes, these values are tied to performance management evaluations to encourage employees to walk the talk. Your values statement communicates the expectations your organization has of its employees.

Charles Schwab[1]

> At Charles Schwab, having a strong brand is a competitive advantage and a strategic advantage. They state, "We rely on our vision and values as the promise and the operating rules we use for our employees. At some level it's part of our brand, but it's more a code of conduct."

However, your organizational values should also serve as a guide on how an employee can expect to be treated by your organization in return. It's one component of an employee brand promise. In today's employee-driven marketplace, the C-suite (CEO, CIO, COO, CFO, etc.), HR professionals, and organizational design leaders are discussing the need to create an employee brand promise that will act as a tool to attract and retain the right people for the right job. The construction, experience, and communication of an employee brand promise parallels that of a customer brand promise designed by marketing departments. Marketers create customer brand promises as a guarantee of a unique product or service experience.

The employee brand promise has the same objective. It's a promise to employees as to the type of experiences they will have—from their first touch point right through their entire career with the organization. The key is to have harmony and congruence between what you offer customers and what you offer employees. "It's a holistic view that understands that no one company can deliver its brand experience consistently in the marketplace without delivering the same experience to employees."[2] This chapter explores the construction, experience, and communication of an employee brand promise, including the benefits and drawbacks, and its ability to differentiate your organization as an employer of choice. Our client work, whether focused specifically on evaluating an employee brand promise or simply improving programs, policies, and practices, helps organizations and managers live their employee brand promise in all their day-to-day actions.

Employee Brand Promise—Construct

The Conference Board defines an employee brand promise as an organization's "values, systems, policies and behaviors toward the objectives of attracting, motivating and retaining . . . current and potential employees."[3] The organization's identity as an employer is thereby created. We simplify the definition: An employee brand promise (EBP) is your total rewards program plus your statement of values.

$$EBP = Total\ rewards + Values$$

In chapter 5, total rewards programs were discussed as a retention mechanism; here, the program is used as a component of an employee brand promise. Total rewards are all the financial and non-financial benefits of working at your organization. The non-financial areas include skill development, career opportunities, and quality of work-life. To equate these HR components in marketing terms, the total rewards components are the "product or services" that your company offers employees. However, the employee brand promise is also the experience of these products. This is where organizational values come into play. Organizational values are the promise of a certain type of experience. For example, if one of your organizational values is integrity, then employees should be treated with integrity in the interview process, in their performance reviews, in being assigned challenging work assignments, or in their interaction with the HR department.

One of the benefits of designing an employee brand promise is that you will attract more desirable candidates. Prospective candidates are able to prejudge whether or not the promise you are offering is one that they want and, conversely, whether or not they can live up to your corporate values. Also, you reduce the risk of early turnover as your entire offer is on the table. Prospective employees know what is expected of them, and they know in return what they can expect from you. For example, Southwest and GE are well-known for having created workplace experiences that live up to their promises. They "provide a special work-environment as a magnet to employees who fit their workforce model—the model that describes the work characteristics of persons that succeed in these businesses."[4]

Employee Brand Promise—Experience

Customer brands are designed to build customer loyalty. Building a strong brand requires two characteristics to be present—recognition and perception.[5] Customers recognize a brand through one of the five senses, the visual being the most dominant. One way to create a positive perception of a brand is through customer experience with the product/service. Employee branding must have the same characteristics. Your organization's employee brand must be recognized and perceived as valuable by all employee groups. If the objective of a successful employee brand is to drive "a commitment to organizational connectivity,"[6] then you want employees to build an affinity to your organization. You want them to believe that they can have a better experience working for your organization than working for your competitor. The key is to differentiate your organization, making your company uniquely attractive, particularly to people who have the knowledge, skills, and attitudes you desire.

Your employee brand should be recognized and perceived as providing a certain quality of experience. Microsoft, IBM, and GE, as employers, have highly recognizable brands in the employee labor market.[7] Their brands can be considered as a type of capital—social capital.[8] Social capital is the value which working for your organization has in the marketplace. The more valuable your social capital, the greater an asset it is to your organization. As an asset, it can help you recruit and retain employees.

Naturally, the greatest potential pitfall of an employee brand promise is inconsistent or weak execution. An EBP is more than just a marketing tool. "You can't just spiff things up and put it on a Web site."[9] In fact, the message must be: we actually live this and do this. There has to be a harmony between what is communicated externally and what is being lived internally. One of the gaps in organizational design is that fantastic people programs, strategies, and policies are created without a plan for consistent execution. Organizations also often don't interconnect the execution of multiple HR programs into a holistic approach. With total rewards, leaders create the framework and the pieces that fit into a program, but often, managers and employees don't know how to consistently execute the components of the program. For example, if your total rewards program includes learning and development opportunities, then managers must have the budget to grant employees access to learning. Often, with budget restrictions, learning and development programs are cut. Unless there is transparent communication about why this has happened and what the next step is, employees will perceive that your organization has broken part of its promise. Organizations which don't measure managers on the successful execution of total rewards programs risk inconsistent delivery of their EBP. The consequence of not measuring or not encouraging delivery on the promise results in a weakened brand.

Southwest[10]

Southwest's employee brand promise provides behavioral guidance. They chose the word *freedom* to demonstrate that employees have active control rather than just being passive recipients.

The "Freedom Begins with Me" campaign includes the following eight freedoms:

- The freedom to pursue good health
- The freedom to create financial security
- The freedom to learn and grow
- The freedom to make a positive difference
- The freedom to travel
- The freedom to work hard and have fun
- The freedom to create and innovate
- The freedom to stay connected

The same applies to knowing how to demonstrate organizational values. Leaders determine the values that the organization stands for. HR designs and distributes posters, key chains, and post lists that define the values. However, managers often don't know how to translate these values into everyday operational actions. If one of your values is customer commitment but one department doesn't meet deliverables, then employees feel that their experience with your organization is inconsistent with your promise to them. This type of reality can lead to a disconnect. While organizations often measure how employees demonstrate corporate values to external customers and vendors, they rarely measure how well the organization demonstrates those same values internally to their employees. Since it's the managers who create the brand experience for employees, they must be clear on how to live the brand promise in their day-to-day actions.

Employee Brand Promise—Communicate

Many organizations participate in best employer lists to advertise the uniqueness of their employee brand promise. While getting on the list helps in creating a positive perception of your organization's social capital, the benefits are quickly lost if your organization doesn't consistently meet the perception of your brand.[11] The best employer lists may help initially in recruiting employees, but they are not helpful in retaining employees. Organizations need to reinforce that they are living up to their employee brand promise constantly and consistently. We would caution against relying on the best employer lists as the primary vehicle of communicating your EBP. "Although it is helpful to have a workplace brand confirmed by a prestigious magazine, the actual branding must cascade from the company's business goals rather than an external source."[12]

At Pfizer, while the messages might be created at the senior corporate level and at the operational divisional level, the messages are amplified and linked to specific strategies and objectives.[13] It is your current workforce that judges whether or not your organization is living up to your brand promise. If you restructure or undergo a change initiative, you need to communicate how you will continue to deliver on your promise going forward. If you can no longer live up to your EBP, then you need to come clean as to why and communicate how your EBP will change. Always over-communicate as key messages are often forgotten if they aren't heard several times.

BASF[14]

BASF, in redesigning its brand for employees, took their external message, "we make things better," and applied it internally. Their employee brand promise states, "We make things better—especially careers." According to employees, BASF provides good opportunities, rewards hard work, and receives high scores on career development.

Since it takes more than just once to communicate your promise, you need an internal communication plan.[15] What's most important is that your messages use the same image and voice that you use to communicate with external customers. The objective is to create the same internal perception of your brand among employees as you have externally with customers. The look and feel of the communication vehicles and content must be consistent.[16] All the materials that are produced by HR—from the benefits guide, to the Web site, to recruiting and training materials—need to communicate the same message. The message is how the program, initiative, or day-to-day activities demonstrate your values and/or deliver on your total rewards program.

Demonstrating Organizational Engagement

It is through the communication of your employee brand promise that your organization demonstrates transparency. Your communication should be clear, precise, and use visuals to show the linkages between a particular strategy/program and the employee brand promise. Since one of the characteristics of a brand is strong recognition, you achieve greater recognition the more visible the connections are between what you are delivering and what employees are receiving. So you should have communication vehicles in place that highlight how your organization is demonstrating its values. The focus should also be on measuring and broadcasting how employees are demonstrating your values, both internally and externally, for example, through newsletters or recognition programs.

The demonstration of your EBP can't be static. Your employee brand promise is responsive if it has been created and modified based on input from employees. Employees are the best group to tap into to learn how the connection between your promise and organizational actions can be made stronger. As your organization merges with, acquires, or sells off businesses or as your demographics change, your employee brand promise should change as well. It might change because certain components of your total rewards program may no longer be necessary or valued.

In executing your employee brand promise, you are demonstrating pure partnership. If the employee brand promise is public—open for all to learn—then your organization is communicating what you are committing to as an employer. By holding up your end of the partnership, you will recruit, retain, and engage your workforce.

Generational Considerations

While the term *employee brand promise* is relatively new, the concept or intent behind the term is not. Historically, most Traditionalists received a promise from their organizations. For most of their careers, there was job security, incremental pay increases, and the opportunity for promotions. While the processes weren't transparent, employees knew what working for one organization or another meant to them in terms of pay, benefits, and stability. The employee promise was pretty consistent across organizations and industries. So Traditionalists and many Baby Boomers might be surprised or even skeptical of the need to have an EBP, to communicate it to employees, and to hold managers accountable for living up to the promise in their day-to-day actions.

Baby Boomers might be skeptical that your organization is committing to any real action and that you will live up to your EBP. When this cohort entered the workplace, in particular the older Boomers, they were offered the standard promise given to Traditionalists. However, since they experienced the broken promises by organizations in the '80s and '90s, Baby Boomers may not actually believe that your organization will ever truly live up to any kind of employee brand promise. With this generation, communication and creating linkages between managerial actions and your EBP is the key. Since a brand is based on perception, Baby Boomers' perception of the value of your employee brand promise needs to be strengthened through consistent action.

Gen Xers value and appreciate an employee brand promise. The clearer it is as to what they can expect from you as an employer, the better. Since this cohort emphasizes their value as investors in your organization, your EBP is one of the ways that they can judge what their return on investment will be by working for you. Also, your employee brand promise quickly tells Gen Xers about your culture and work environment. Gen Xers will judge in advance whether your social capital is an asset to them or not. For existing Gen X employees, living up to the brand promise through everyday actions, decisions, and activities is the key to retaining them. The more they feel that there are multiple infractions of the promise, the more likely they are to disengage.

Similar to Gen Xers, Gen Ys expect you to have an employee brand promise, but they expect it to be very clear and objective as to the benefits they will receive. That's the goal behind many of the questions asked by Gen Ys during the interview process and discussed with managers post-hire. Gen Ys also expect a consistent and fair application of your EBP across all functions and levels. They shouldn't perceive that the executive team demonstrates or lives up to the EBP differently than employees. Both Gen Xers and Gen Ys have a need for speed; meaning, they will not give managers or your organizations a long time to live up to your promise. Any infraction, even for a good reason, needs to be acknowledged, addressed, and corrected. As we mentioned previously, it may be all right to break the promise, but the acknowledgement and the new plan announcement are the keys to maintaining engagement levels.

Metrics That Matter

Some examples of quantitative metrics you can use to evaluate the success of your employee brand promise include the following:

- ✌ Engagement surveys related to your organization's execution of your employee brand promise
- ✌ Recognition of your employee brand promise by prospective candidates and employees
- ✌ Key message recognition
- ✌ Demonstration of corporate values through observable behaviors by managers and employees

Sample Engagement Survey—Employee Brand Promise (EBP)

Transparency demonstrated by specific, accurate, and open communication

- ☐ Can employees state in two or three sentences your EBP?
- ☐ Does your EBP communicate what type of employee will be successful in your organization?
- ☐ Are all HR strategies linked to your EBP?

Responsiveness demonstrated by timeliness and feedback

- ☐ Do employees have an evaluation mechanism to judge whether the organization is living up to its EBP?
- ☐ Do you have a mechanism in place in the event your EBP is broken at the managerial or organizational level?
- ☐ Do you share stories about how your EBP is demonstrated day-to-day?

Partnering demonstrated by the organization/managers collaborating with employees

- ☐ Can employees hold managers accountable for demonstrating your EBP?
- ☐ Do managers and employees discuss how to live the EBP in their day-to-day actions?
- ☐ Do managers have a framework to translate your organizational values into day-to-day operational activities?

*   *While these questions are based on a yes/no response, a Likert scale may provide richer data, depending on the size and complexity of your organization. Be sure to analyze data along demographic lines as well.*

Section IV

How to Grow 'Em

Developing employees is a key mechanism to retaining employees, but for many organizations, it is also a business strategy. Talent management is not just training or learning and development, it includes career-pathing, mentoring, and performance management as well. If your organization doesn't have a well-constructed talent management strategy that is linked to business outcomes, then you don't have a sustainable plan for growing your business in the future. "Among all of the factors that could influence the effectiveness of (your) organization in the future, the foremost driver is talent."[1] A successful talent management strategy aligns talent practices to business requirements. It makes sure that each talent component integrates with one another across the employee life cycle. That means your ability to manage your talent has a direct impact on your recruitment, retention, and succession-planning success.

The most successful organizations create a talent management strategy that is characterized by the following:[2]

- ✌ Is linked to business strategy and key priorities
- ✌ Is supported and championed by senior leadership
- ✌ Communicates who is and who isn't top talent[3]
- ✌ Moves people into new roles before they are ready
- ✌ Minimizes managers' ability to hoard talent
- ✌ Embeds talent management practices across the organization as an integral part of doing business

A comprehensive talent management strategy requires that an organization place as much importance on the acquisition, development, and management of talent as it does on other corporate assets. It's about creating an organizational mindset where talent management practices cut across businesses, geographies, and silos. It becomes the responsibility of all leaders, where "one stops to think about the implication of talent before making major business decisions."[4]

Making an investment in creating a comprehensive talent management strategy drives organizational results by:[5]

- ❖ Supporting employee growth and success through a clear career-pathing process

- ❖ Developing employee capabilities required to execute and achieve business strategy

- ❖ Aligning employee performance expectations with organizational goals

- ❖ Integrating pay, performance, and career development program in order to improve retention and increase employee engagement

In this section, we will discuss six building blocks of an effective talent management strategy. They are the following:

Career-pathing	providing employees with a road map for career growth
Learning and development	maximizing the transfer of learning back on the job and driving business outcomes through varied programs and experiences
Mentoring	facilitating one-on-one relationships between mentors and mentees with the purpose of providing advice, direction, and guidance
Performance management	communicating, tracking, and rewarding individual performance
Succession planning	executing a four-point succession-planning process to identify and move employees within your organization
Management practices	cultivating a management style that motivates and engages all employee groups

Chapter Seven

Career-pathing: Show Me The
Possibilities and Don't Block My Path

Developing clear, concise career paths for employees plays a critical role throughout the employee life cycle—from recruitment and retention to succession planning. If employees can understand where they currently are in your organization and, more importantly, where they can go, then they are likely to be more engaged and more committed. Our commitment is to ensure that there is clarity around the career options our clients offer their employees. This helps managers make better decisions regarding promotions, succession planning, and compensation.

With the demands of rapid career changes and a desire for cross-functional experiences, employees today are eager to have a road map for success. Today's career paths are more spiral than linear, requiring that employees apply their knowledge and skills to a variety of roles. Developing spiral career paths helps all employees to proactively participate in their own career development. The career path demonstrates to employees the opportunities for growth over the long term. They create a common language for defining role expectations for jobs at different organizational levels.[1]

They identify role requirements such as accountabilities and business and technical knowledge requirements, as well as soft skill behaviors. These role requirements are described for each functional level on the career path, illustrating how the requirements become more complex as employees progress into more senior roles. The different paths (or levels) are defined through a combination of existing job descriptions and required competency levels. Existing jobs are then mapped to various career paths, using the description of the role's accountability to guide the placement of the job on the path.[2] This framework paints a picture of the organization and how roles evolve in terms of performance expectations and complexity. The framework allows for meaningful discussions between managers and employees about career aspirations and development needs.

When career paths are created for multiple functional areas, they help encourage lateral and cross-functional moves. They highlight how employees can transfer their skills to another area of the business where their level of accountability would be the same. A successful career-pathing strategy should promote cross-functional moves, including geographic relocation such as global assignments.

Boehringer Ingelheim[3]

When the pharmaceutical company Boehringer Ingelheim experienced rapid growth and expansion, it realized that there is a need for a concerted effort on developing and growing internal talent to meet new demanding business needs. They created their "On Track to Success" program, a career pathway, and leadership development model. It was initially targeted at the sales role and was later rolled out to all employees. By providing career ladders for key roles, employees can identify growth opportunities by reviewing competencies and job descriptions for each step in the ladder. The program is highly transparent, encouraging employees to self assess their current abilities against future career aspirations. In addition, the program is closely tied to the organization's learning and development, and performance management processes. This creates a culture where internal talent is continuously developed and coached, as an investment in the organization's long-term success.

All role descriptions, accountabilities, and knowledge requirements should include your organization's key competencies—at an organizational, divisional, and individual level. Competencies usually refer to the knowledge, abilities/skills, and personal qualities required to deliver superior performance.[4] For example, organizations typically identify management/leadership competencies that encompass a wide range of behaviors such as demonstrating the corporate values, operational excellence, business acumen, teamwork, valuing diversity, and being client focused. We recommend that to further ensure a common understanding of role requirements between managers and employees, each competency must be transformed into observable behaviors (OBs). OBs are precise, objective statements that describe how employees demonstrate competency within their role. The intent of observable behaviors is to eliminate subjectivity during the evaluation process since managers, peers, and reports can assess whether or not they observe the desired behavior. For example, an observable behavior of being client focused would be to ask for feedback from customers. Given this criteria, a manager can assess employees' behaviors while providing an opportunity for employees to also self-evaluate their performance.

By providing objective OBs, employees can/will have a better understanding as to what is expected of them in their roles. Managers can use the OBs as a basis for performance assessments and discussions of developmental needs. The more precise and detailed your OBs, the clearer the requirements for promotions and career advancement are. By providing a road map, linked to career growth, both managers and employees can objectively measure performance and identify the next steps.

Demonstrating Organizational Engagement

By helping employees to navigate their careers—both within and beyond your organization—you will strengthen your employment relationship and demonstrate a commitment to creating a win-win outcome. You are demonstrating transparency and partnering in that employees can clearly map out their potential career growth, as well as being able to take the initiative to collaborate with their manager on ways to get them there. Being responsive to your employees also requires that you provide career-pathing options that align to their wants and desires, not just where your organization has a gap or need. Managers that can respond to employees' career aspirations by providing a variety of experiences will have more motivated and engaged employees. The organization benefits as a whole by promoting internal growth and development.

Generational Considerations

Each generation has different expectations of the type of guidance your organization should provide. Traditionalists may initially be uncomfortable identifying where they can grow within your organization. Many in this cohort (and Baby Boomers as well) have experienced a top-down approach to career development, where senior leaders directed the employees' next move. However, with open communication and support for the development of new skills, Traditionalists are able to leverage your career-pathing process to identify where and how they can have the greatest impact on the organization by leaving a legacy. Traditionalists may desire a lateral move to another part of the organization, where their expertise can be utilized, or be placed on a special assignment to act as a coach or advisor.

For experienced Baby Boomers, they appreciate your dedication to them by demonstrating, through a career path, where they currently are within your organization and where they can go. This helps reengage long-term employees who may feel they have reached a plateau and allows those in the middle of their career to identify new paths. Baby Boomers are now concerned with career growth that is meaningful. While they have dedicated the first part of their careers to acquiring material and financial success, many are "willing to trade some of their current success for greater significance in their lives and work, even if that means doing something altogether different."[5]

All generations want opportunities to grow and develop. However, the younger generations bring a high level of expectation for career opportunities that are varied, cross-functional, and earlier in their careers. Given Gen Xers' desire to gain marketable skills, a detailed career-pathing process appeals to this generation. It helps to identify a variety of possibilities of where they can go within the organization and what they need to do to realize their career goals. While Baby Boomers and Traditionalists may have been accustomed to having their career paths defined and directed for them, Gen Xers and Gen Ys expect to manage their careers themselves. They don't believe in, nor trust, an organization to look after them.

By clearly identifying observable behaviors as part of your career paths, you will be appealing to Gen Ys' sense of fair play and equity and to Gen Xers' desire for objectivity. When younger employees can assess their current skill level—through self-assessment and manager/peer feedback—they can better identify gaps in their performance. Those gaps can then be closed by taking the initiative to learn new skills or demonstrate different behaviors. Also, given that Gen Ys have a need for speed, career paths that not only allow but promote cross-functional moves will align to this generation's motivations and expectations. This allows employees to move into a variety of different roles at a relatively quick pace. It's a win-win situation for both employees and the organization. Spiral career paths build bench strength for the organization through depth and breadth of experience and provide enough variety to keep Gen Ys engaged, excited, and motivated. As part of the win-win employment relationship, Gen X and Gen Y employees expect you to offer formal career paths as proof of your commitment to them.

Metrics That Matter

Some examples of quantitative metrics you can use to evaluate your career-pathing process are the following:

- Retention rates
- Promotions by level
- Promotions by each generation
- Employees' demonstration of key competencies and OBs within their role
- Speed of career growth
- Number of cross-functional positions created/filled
- Number of complete, accurate job descriptions with observable behaviors
- Number of lateral moves
- Employee engagement scores on questions related to growth and development opportunities and future growth opportunities

Sample Engagement Survey—Career-pathing

Transparency demonstrated by specific, accurate, and open communication

- ☐ Do employees understand where their career can grow within your organization?
- ☐ Do you encourage lateral, cross-functional, and global assignments for all employees?
- ☐ Can employees state the competencies and observable behaviors required for their current and future roles?

Responsiveness demonstrated by timeliness and feedback

- ☐ Do employees understand the typical timeline for a career path in your organization?
- ☐ Can employees influence the speed of their career path?
- ☐ Can employees talk to HR about where their careers may lead?

Partnering demonstrated by the organization/managers collaborating with employees

- ☐ Are managers held accountable for making their employees' career goals come to life?
- ☐ Can employees create new and alternative career paths to meet their individual career goals?
- ☐ Do managers encourage employees to consider/apply fo jobs outside of their own department?

*   *While these questions are based on a yes/no response, a Likert scale may provide richer data, depending on the size and complexity of your organization. Be sure to analyze data along demographic lines as well.*

Chapter Eight

Learning and Development:
Learning as My Ticket to Marketability

Once you have clearly outlined your career paths, your learning and development plans should be aligned to support them. Learning and development initiatives help support your organization's career-pathing process by providing employees with opportunities for formal and informal learning experiences. The experiences help employees either to improve performance in their current role or to develop the competencies required for future career opportunities. For the system to work well, employees must take the initiative to complete individual learning and development plans. Also, managers must be prepared and skilled in conducting developmental conversations.

General Mills[1]

General Mills has developed a process where managers and employees discuss development plans formally between June and August as well as ongoing throughout the year. These discussions are separate from the annual performance review process as there is a strong belief that "you can't have a development discussion and an appraisal discussion at the same time."

Developmental discussions at General Mills focus on four key areas:

1. Professional goals/motivations—Where do employees want to go in their career?
2. Talents or strengths to use more—What are they?
3. Development opportunities—What needs are important to improve?
4. Focused development objectives and action steps—What employee objectives and actions will be taken to achieve them?

It is through learning and development programs that employees can acquire the knowledge, skills, and attitudes required for success. Learning and development may be formal such as classroom workshops, e-learning, or on-the-job assignments or informal such as peer sharing, lunch and learns, or communities of practice. The success of your learning and development program (or training) is measured by its ability to impact individual and business performance. The objective is to focus on knowledge, skills, and attitudes that improve organizational effectiveness and increase employee effectiveness. Learning and development initiatives need to focus on where your business is headed, not on where it is currently.

Learning is maximized when employees understand how the knowledge and skills developed in a program are linked to their current role and future job possibilities. "Trainees who are confident they can succeed in training, who see the training as relevant to their jobs or careers, and who value the outcome of training (i.e., see learning as useful) are more motivated in training."[2] By being clear on how the learning helps achieve business objectives, employees can create a linkage between the content and results.

Another major factor in the success of transferring learning to on-the-job performance is the work environment, including manager support. A work environment that supports learning provides employees with opportunities to practice the new skills. Management support for learning and development is critical for long-term skills enhancement and development effectiveness. Your organization can have the best learning and development programs, but if the post-learning environment doesn't support and encourage the transfer of new skills, your efforts will be in vain.

Many organizations recognize the value that on-the-job learning or action-learning plays in increasing training effectiveness. "It's far more effective to pair classroom training with real-life exposure to a variety of jobs and bosses, such as using techniques like job rotation, special assignments . . . and action learning."[3] The goal is to effectively and quickly transfer new skills back on the job. To achieve this, we help clients create action-learning programs that require employees to complete assignments within their everyday work environment as part of their learning. The future of learning and development is likely to shift from individual-oriented learning toward more team-based learning (virtual and global) where employees are required to work together to achieve a common goal. In this type of learning environment, technology-based learning becomes even more important in helping learners to share information, collaborate, and learn. Workplace learning will become more integrated into our daily workflow, and technology will facilitate improved workplace performance. Working and learning will be a seamless experience.[4]

One of the most effective action-learning experiences is an intrapreneurship program that brings a cross-functional group of people together to solve a real business challenge. The objective is to tap into the entrepreneurial spirit within your organization. It's a way of harnessing creativity, innovativeness, and competitiveness for the good of your organization. In many cases, intrapreneurship programs involve pulling together a group of high-potential employees (though the program can also be more broadly used to target the masses) to study and make recommendations on an up-and-coming strategic business issue.[5] In our experience, intrapreneurship programs serve a dual purpose. First, they provide a developmental experience for employees and deepen networks across the organization by connecting a variety of colleagues from different functional areas. Learners step out of their own silos to create holistic solutions to strategic business issues. Second, this type of program generates useful work product for the company, which translates into improved business performance.

American Express[6]

When AMEX implemented their intrapreneurship program targeted at high-potential middle managers, they incorporated formal classroom learning with action-learning. The action-learning component of the program has cross-functional teams working to identify real business opportunities. The organization has used the program to broaden its talent base from which to draw the next generation of leaders. It's a win-win outcome: employees strengthen their networks and the organization "gets different thinking [which] compliments and supplements what our executives are doing."

Demonstrating Organizational Engagement

In order to create a positive learning environment, managers should:

- ❧ Understand the relationship between the learning content and the competencies required for the employee's current role and future career aspirations
- ❧ Meet with employees before they attend training to discuss the learning and development goals and the importance of the training and to understand the employee's expectations
- ❧ Support the learning by providing opportunities to apply and practice new skills
- ❧ Provide coaching and feedback on new skills

These management techniques demonstrate transparency, responsiveness, and partnering. Being transparent about how learning and development programs contribute to both individual and team success helps employees understand the role they play in improving their skills for the benefit of their career growth and the team's performance. Coaching, feedback, and opportunities to practice new skills demonstrate responsiveness when managers adjust the work environment to support learning. Understanding employees' goals and supporting their growth create a partnering relationship between your organization and employees, which reinforces your organization's commitment to a collaborative relationship.

Generational Considerations

The four generations hold different expectations of learning content and application. For Traditionalists, learning has typically focused on technical/functional skills, not broader people management abilities. Also, it was often directed and mandated by the organization. For your experienced workers, consider providing them with a list of suggested learning; then have them identify the direction they would like their development to go. For many Traditionalists, skill development opportunities may focus on technology or new business applications.

Baby Boomers are motivated to participate in learning and development initiatives where learning outcomes link to their specific development plans, which may lead to job promotions. This cohort is eager to remain in the know; they want exposure to learning that allows them to add value to your organization, raise their profile by being an expert, and remain on the cutting edge of industry trends.

Your Gen X employees have a baseline expectation that, as an employer, you will invest in their development. This includes formal learning programs such as in-house training or off-site programs, tuition reimbursement, and cross-functional assignments. Gen Xers want to be able to gain marketable skills by working on stretch assignments, participating in intrapreneurship programs, and interacting with global colleagues through communities of practice. This cohort views learning and development as the most important investment that you can make to create a win-win employment relationship with them. They want learning experiences that focus on problem solving and results, not theory, so that they can improve their marketability and performance on the job.

Since Gen Ys have been exposed to a wide variety of learning—from classroom to computer software games and online simulations—this generation expects that workplace learning will be engaging and fun. The concept of *edutainment* is blending *edu*cation with enter*tainment* to create a learning environment that transfers knowledge in a fun way. Most appealing to this cohort is learning initiatives that help them gain skills that not only make them more marketable in the future, but directly impact their ability to earn more money in their current roles. They desire learning experiences that incorporate technology, allow for collaboration with peers, and help translate new skills into immediate results.

Metrics That Matter

Some examples of quantitative metrics you can use to evaluate your learning and development initiatives are the following:

- ✌ Participation rates in formal learning
- ✌ Knowledge transfer back on the job (using Kirkpatrick level 2, 3, and 4 measurement tools and Jack Phillips level 5 ROI)
- ✌ Key performance indicators—financial targets, customer satisfaction, shareholder value
- ✌ Link between individual performance management rating and participation in learning and development
- ✌ Number of new solutions/innovative ideas generated
- ✌ Completion of individual development plans

Sample Engagement Survey—Learning and Development

Transparency demonstrated by specific, accurate, and open communication

- ☐ Are learning outcomes linked to strategic goals and individual roles?

- ☐ Are learning and development programs/initiatives linked to career paths?

- ☐ Do all employees have access and knowledge of your learning and development opportunities/programs?

Responsiveness demonstrated by timeliness and feedback

- ☐ Can employees select learning and development experiences that align to their career goals?

- ☐ Do all learning opportunities involve a budget?

- ☐ Do you ask employees what learning experiences they would like your organization to offer?

Partnering demonstrated by the organization/managers collaborating with employees

- ☐ Do employees identify their own learning and development needs/wants?

- ☐ Do managers actively encourage learning?

- ☐ Do managers co-participate in learning activities?

* *While these questions are based on a yes/no response, a Likert scale may provide richer data, depending on the size and complexity of your organization. Be sure to analyze data along demographic lines as well.*

Chapter Nine

Mentoring: Be My Guide on the Side
and Not the Sage on the Stage

Based on employees' career paths and individual development plans, it may be helpful for them to participate in a mentorship program to expand their knowledge and expertise and provide guidance from a more seasoned colleague. Typically, a mentoring relationship is focused less on technical knowledge, which can be learned through developmental programs, but more on information and advice that helps with career development. The mentoring relationship can both enhance employees' career development and assist with psycho-social functions such as acceptance, emotional support, and role-modeling. In a study of mentees at a large global corporation, it was found that 65 percent valued the career-orientation aspect (e.g., extending networks) of the mentoring relationship and 47 percent valued the psycho-social functions (e.g., friendly and compassionate). The two most important factors valued in a mentor were experience and respect. For some mentees, respect was defined as "mutual respect," meaning, respect for their opinions and values, and for others, it was based more on admiration.[1]

Many of our clients have developed formal mentorship programs in an effort to reduce turnover and improve overall corporate performance. They view mentorship programs as a key driver in attracting and retaining high-performance employees. "Mentorship programs are one way of demonstrating to high potentials that the organization has a commitment to their future and is willing to take steps to help them achieve their career goals."[2]

Formal mentorship programs typically include an orientation/training program for both mentors and mentees. The intent is to outline expectations and responsibilities of both parties, the content and frequency of mentorship meetings, and the confidentiality of the discussions. In some cases, mentors may be assigned employees or employees may be able to select mentors based on best fit and mutual interests.[3] The most successful mentoring relationships are the ones where mentors don't provide performance feedback, but rather act as a sounding board to help employees problem-solve. Mentoring programs should be continuously monitored to ensure both parties are benefiting from the relationship. If the relationship isn't working out, realignment may be required to ensure that the objectives of the program, mentor, and mentee are being met.

Reverse mentoring is a relatively new spin on the mentoring relationship. It's often more informal and involves mentees providing their mentor with knowledge or advice. In some cases, the objective may be to focus on the use of technology or the integration of technology into workflow processes. Mentees may also provide feedback to their mentors on their performance as a mentor/leader by recommending areas for improvement as it relates to people management skills. When constructing mentoring programs, we provide opportunities for reverse mentoring because it facilitates bottom-up communication and helps mentors remain grounded. "As years go by, we can get out of touch and this keeps us in tune to the concerns of young professionals."[4]

Bell Canada[5]

> Bell Canada, has implemented an online mentorship program branded "Mentor Match". It matches mentees with an appropriate mentor from a cross-sectional pool of potential candidates. The program allows mentees to fill out an online profile, stating their goals, competencies, and career history. Once submitted, "the system searches available mentor profiles and generates a list of top ten possible matches." The mentee then selects who they would like to work with and sends a request, which the mentor can accept or decline. Should there be a match, both parties are prompted to complete a formal one-year mentoring contract. To support the mentor-mentee relationship, there is a four-hour online program available that focuses on how to be an effective mentor or mentee. The program incorporates traditional top-down mentoring, as well as peer-to-peer and reverse mentoring. As a result, mentoring has become embedded in Bell Canada's culture as a way of doing business.

Demonstrating Organizational Engagement

A mentoring program that demonstrates the characteristics of organizational engagement is transparent about the program's motives and objectives (e.g., reduce retention or transfer knowledge), as well as the role of both the mentor and mentee. It's responsive to experienced employees' expectations for participating in mentorship opportunities. It also meets the expectations of younger employees (particularly Gen Ys) of wanting to connect with senior people within the organization. Partnering is promoted by reverse mentoring as it demonstrates respect and value for both the mentor and mentee, regardless of title, seniority, or tenure. The relationship is also partnering as both parties view themselves as equal members of the mentoring team.

Generational Considerations

How you structure your mentorship program and evaluate its success is influenced by which generational motivations and expectations you want to address. The old model of mentoring, based on senior managers providing direction to a subordinate/protégé, was used primarily as a succession-planning and knowledge-transfer tool. The objective was for senior leaders to pass on their knowledge and shape young protégés in their image. It was typically a one-sided, top-down relationship, where protégés were expected to learn everything they could from their role models, becoming just like them. This model of mentoring was usually reserved for only a few employees who were selected to assume leadership positions. This is the model that most Traditionalists and many Baby Boomers experienced. Today's more collaborative approach to mentoring, which includes reverse mentoring, requires that Traditionalist mentors be open to receiving feedback. The mentors acknowledge that their role as a mentor is to assist mentees in realizing goals and aspirations. Mentorship opportunities are a great way for Traditionalists to give back to the organization and pass on their knowledge. Traditionalist mentees may feel awkward providing bottom-up feedback to their mentor given their strong respect for hierarchy and seniority. Also, they may look to mentors to behave in the old model. They may be hesitant to voice their desires for a mentoring relationship. This cohort needs to be encouraged to voice their goals and expectations so that they are met by a formal mentorship program.

Baby Boomer employees are eager to participate as mentors since this provides them with an opportunity to share their experience and skills. Mentorship opportunities are a great way to maximize Baby Boomers' strength of creating collaborative dialogue. Again, the caution is to ensure that mentors don't overpower mentorship conversations by directing mentees on what they *should* do or how they *should* solve problems. A successful mentor is one that helps mentees self-identify how they can succeed. As mentees, Baby Boomers are most motivated when they are paired with a prominent, successful mentor. They are more open than their younger colleagues to listening to war stories and anecdotes of the past from their mentors. Stories that highlight skills and attitudes for success that they can apply in their roles resonate with them.

Based on Gen Xers' need to remain independent and focus on competencies, they are most motivated when they have the option to select their own mentor. They need to feel that their mentor is competent as this allows them to learn from that person. Also, they want to select mentors who demonstrate mutual respect through two-way dialogue focused on solving problems and achieving results rather than storytelling. A top-down maternal or paternal mentoring relationship doesn't engage Gen Xers. This cohort is open to providing feedback as part of reverse mentoring as long as the objective is to improve the mentoring relationship. As mentors, this cohort needs to acknowledge that some mentees desire a collaborative relationship that is focused on more than just problem solving.

Since they are just at the beginning of their careers, Gen Ys today are almost exclusively mentees. This generation is much more open to mentoring than Gen Xers, given their exposure to peer learning in the classroom, a collaborative relationship with their parents, and strong bond with their traditionalist grandparents. Gen Ys are motivated by a formal mentorship program that is tied to career-pathing. It becomes a resource to help them progress more quickly in their careers. This cohort enthusiastically participates in reverse mentoring, particularly when they can use their technological know-how to help their mentor use the latest and greatest programs/applications. Gen Ys view the mentor-mentee relationship as a peer relationship where they can freely share their opinions, ideas, and suggestions for improvement. A mentorship program that is centered on both parties sharing ideas has the greatest appeal to this cohort.

Metrics That Matter

Some examples of quantitative metrics you can use to evaluate your mentorship program are the following:

- Retention rates
- Improved individual performance
- Success of the mentor-mentee relationship
- Length of mentoring relationship
- Integration of new employees into the corporate culture
- Knowledge transfer
- Speed to competency for new hires/new promotions
- Impact on recruitment—importance of mentorship opportunities to candidates

Sample Engagement Survey—Mentoring

Transparency demonstrated by specific, accurate, and open communication

☐ Are the objectives of your mentorship program understood by both mentors and mentees?

☐ Do mentors and mentees understand their roles and accountabilities?

☐ Is the selection process clear to all?

Responsiveness demonstrated by timeliness and feedback.

☐ Does your mentorship program involve experienced employees who want to participate?

☐ Do mentors and mentees regularly provide feedback on the benefits of the mentorship program and how it can be improved?

☐ Do you have a mechanism in place to deal with a mentoring relationship that isn't working well?

Partnering demonstrated by the organization/managers collaborating with employees

☐ Does your mentorship program encourage/promote reverse mentoring?

☐ Do mentors and mentees set the objectives and goals for the relationship together?

☐ Can mentees select their own mentor?

* *While these questions are based on a yes/no response, a Likert scale may provide richer data, depending on the size and complexity of your organization. Be sure to analyze data along demographic lines as well.*

Chapter Ten

Performance Management: The Objective Framework that Measures Our Win-Win Relationship

At a strategic level, your performance management process should align employee performance with key business objectives. This means:[1]

- Translating key drivers of business performance into actions/decisions/behaviors employees need to demonstrate
- Differentiating employees based on their performance
- Engaging all managers and employees in improving organizational performance

To ensure that employees are clear about how they contribute to organizational performance, your organization should provide "employees with a clear line of sight as to how their actions help or hinder the company's results."[2] According to a study of the best performance management practices, goals aren't simply created at the top and then pushed down throughout the organization. Instead, managers must cascade each level of the organization's goals based on those established for the level directly above.[3] This process empowers employees to help identify where they can add the greatest value to the organization. It creates a free flow of communication about your organizational strategy, goals, and objectives. "An important consequence of the goal flow-down process, and improving the line of sight (for employees), is that information is no longer power because information becomes a commodity in the company."[4] Employees who understand what they need to do (behaviors/ actions/tasks) to make your business more successful are armed with the information they need to make smart decisions.[5] Our work establishes processes to ensure both managers and employees understand their accountability in achieving, evaluating, and discussing performance.

Once corporate goals have been established and trickled down throughout the organization, it's important to establish accountability at an individual level. Performance standards are determined, and a formal performance management process is clearly communicated. For individual accountability to take root, your organization must set clear performance expectations, measure performance, and communicate the rewards and consequences of good and poor performance.[6] Effective performance management motivates high performers to remain on track since they feel that their efforts are being recognized. It persuades poor performers to improve since there are negative outcomes if they don't adjust their behavior.

Digital Education Provider

At a digital education provider, their performance management process creates a structure for communication between managers and employees, to identify developmental goals and opportunities and to understand employee direction and level of ambition. The instrument allows management to express satisfaction and encouragement for the efforts of high-performance employees, and to establish performance improvement plans. The objectives of the communication are to:

Define the goals and expectations as presented in the past review or current job description.

Describe the behaviors that achieve or fail to meet those expectations.

Illustrate the description by citing examples—positive or negative.

Evaluate the employee's performance against the expectation based on the behaviors.

Explain the resulting rating.

Identify goals for the coming year.

Summarize results of the review period and expectations for the coming year.

Question for understanding.

Some managers are using the instrument as a mechanism for employee self-reflection though it shouldn't be a replacement to the manager completing the instrument.

Managers are accountable for collecting objective data on their employees' performance. Ideally, competency descriptors and observable behaviors are created for all employee roles and form the framework of a performance evaluation. The competencies and observable behaviors describe *how* the employee should achieve their performance goals. If gaps exist, your learning and development and coaching programs should act as the framework from which managers and employees can create a performance improvement plan. Measurement and tracking of performance ought to be an ongoing process. Throughout the year, performance discussions should take place to reinforce employees' accountabilities, clarify goals, and review the support required to succeed. Both managers and employees should be on the same page, mutually agreeing on the employees' results and performance rating. At the end of the year, there shouldn't be any surprises.

The performance feedback process need not be unnecessarily contentious or difficult if both managers and employees enter the conversation with a collaborative mindset. Then the evaluation and rating of an employee's performance level can be agreed upon clearly. Also, employees should be encouraged to track their own performance throughout the year. By regularly completing self-assessments, they are better prepared to review their successes and challenges with their manager.

Demonstrating Organizational Engagement

Holding managers accountable for objectively measuring employee performance through regular feedback communicates to employees your commitment to a transparent performance management process. Managers play a pivotal role in communicating and translating strategy into role clarity for their employees. They must provide clear, transparent communication about performance expectations and organizational goals, as well as how performance assessments influence salary, bonus, and career-promotion decisions. To respond to employees' needs for greater feedback regarding their performance, managers should conduct frequent, informal performance discussions to ensure the final year-end performance rating isn't a surprise. An objective system is also responsive to employees' needs and establishes a partnering relationship by engaging them in their own performance measurement. Employees hold increasing accountability in demonstrating a partnering approach. By completing a self-evaluation of strengths and areas of development, employees identify where they can add the greatest value to the organization. The more you engage employees in the process, the more your organization achieves greater commitment to accomplishing results.

Generational Considerations

Based fundamentally on their desire and comfort level with receiving feedback, each generation responds to the performance management process differently.

For most Traditionalists, they experienced a work environment where the only performance feedback given was either really good news, "You're getting promoted!" or really bad news, "You're getting fired!" This generation has only recently been exposed to organizational cultures where ongoing feedback and setting objectives for their performance is the norm. It can sometimes be difficult for Traditionalists to adapt to this new approach since they have been working for many years, sometimes at senior levels, without any formal performance management. An annual performance review process matches the comfort level for this cohort. If they want more feedback, they'll ask for it.

Since the widespread use of performance management metrics isn't that old, for many Baby Boomers, it feels like recent exposure to formal performance reviews. In the past, their performance was often commented on by senior leaders in a more informal way. Rewards were often largely based on the subjective perceptions of contribution by leaders (who you knew) rather than the objective measurement of contribution to business outcomes (what you did). This approach sometimes left out strong performers who didn't play the political game, with little acknowledgement or recognition for their contributions. On the flip side, poor performers who were well connected within the organization were allowed to remain or were even promoted. The performance management process was secretive. It didn't necessarily provide employees with a clear understanding of why their performance was above or below standard.

Often, Baby Boomers enjoy talking about their successes/strengths but are reluctant to express areas of weakness for fear that this will jeopardize their position within the organization. Historically, performance discussions with Baby Boomer employees focused on what they have accomplished and achieved (their wins), followed by feedback on areas of development/improvement, followed by a positive summary on how they are contributing to organizational and departmental goals. This sandwich model of feedback—positive, negative, positive—ensured that performance discussions were positive in tone and didn't become conflict conversations. A formal performance management process that is done annually or bi-annually matches the comfort level of this cohort.

In contrast, Gen X employees want to receive feedback on their performance on a quarterly or monthly basis. Also, they don't want to focus on what they do well—they already know that—they want to understand how they can improve. Managers should provide Gen Xers with:

- ✌ Specific examples of what you would like them to improve on and when
- ✌ How you both will measure success
- ✌ What resources and support you will provide them

The desire for this type of feedback is because of the fact that Gen Xers want to remain marketable, they know they must continuously improve, learn, and grow. Performance discussions should focus on desired results from the managers' and employees' perspectives, as well as be linked to career goals and individual development plans.

Gen Ys are even more eager to receive formal feedback. They want to know how they are performing on a monthly, weekly, and daily basis. Though this generation has a large appetite for feedback, they are often ill prepared to receive negative feedback. Growing up in a school system and home life with high expectations, this generation fears failure. Also, this cohort has always received positive, self-esteem building praise by parents, teachers, and coaches on an ongoing basis. They haven't been accustomed to receiving negative feedback, nor are they well prepared on how to respond. So receiving less than 100 percent on a performance rating may cause an emotional response in some Gen Ys. Managers should be trained to conduct performance discussions with Gen Ys that highlight developmental opportunities without plummeting motivation and engagement levels.

Like Gen Xers, Gen Ys also demand that their performance ratings be objectively quantified to ensure fairness and equality. Given how freely this generation shares information, managers are often taken aback when two Gen Ys want to discuss their performance reviews together. If both employees worked on the same project and both were told that they did a good job, they will want to know why one of them received a higher performance rating (and possibly greater merit increase) than the other. While this situation alone might make some managers cringe, the interesting new twist is that the employee with the *higher* performance rating is the one who is upset that his/her colleague didn't get an equally high rating. This employee will argue that it's not fair that his/her colleague didn't receive the same treatment as s/he did. To handle this type of performance discussion, a manager has to be able to justify their performance ratings with objective, clear data that links to competencies, observable behaviors, and business outcomes. Also, managers should be prepared and open to having these types of discussions with Gen Y employees. Refusing to engage in a conversation about performance leads to employee disengagement and mistrust.

Metrics That Matter

Some examples of quantitative metrics you can use to evaluate your performance management process are the following:

- ✓ Frequency of performance discussions
- ✓ Ability of employees to communicate how their performance goals link to corporate goals
- ✓ Employees' completion of self-evaluations of their performance
- ✓ Level of success in achieving individual performance goals
- ✓ Level of success in achieving organizational performance goals
- ✓ Managers' completion of the performance management process
- ✓ Number of employees rated at each performance level—distinction between high and low performers

Sample Engagement Survey—Performance Management

Transparency demonstrated by specific, accurate, and open communication

☐ Are performance goals cascaded down through your organization?

☐ Can employees link their performance goals with business objectives?

☐ Are employees clear on how their performance will be measured and rewarded?

Responsiveness demonstrated by timeliness and feedback

☐ Are employees' desires for more frequent, informal performance discussions met?

☐ Are employees encouraged to provide feedback to their manager on their performance?

☐ Is feedback from multiple sources incorporated into employee and manager performance evaluations?

Partnering demonstrated by the organization/managers collaborating with employees

☐ Are employees involved in setting their performance goals?

☐ Do employees provide self-assessments, feedback, and sign-off on their performance rating?

☐ Are individual goals linked to your business drivers and desired outcomes?

* *While these questions are based on a yes/no response, a Likert scale may provide richer data, depending on the size and complexity of your organization. Be sure to analyze data along demographic lines as well.*

Chapter Eleven

Succession Planning: If We Can't Move Them Up, Let's Move Them Over

Succession planning is a business issue keeping not only HR leaders, but also C-suite leaders up at night. Some organizations worry about losing a high percentage of employees to retirement in the next few years. Most realize that they can no longer assume that employees will stay with them for the long term, and therefore, their succession plans must be flexible and adaptable to turnover. Couple these issues with an aging workforce and younger employees with more demanding career expectations and you are faced with a distinct challenge. How do you create a succession plan that works and can be sustained? We have presented and assessed in conjunction with organizational leaders which model is best for their current and desired future culture, and whether or not their current plan is sustainable and aligns with business objectives.

The good news is if your organization already has a robust talent and performance management system, then you are well positioned to create a successful succession plan. Succession planning doesn't exist independently. In fact, succession planning "touches all aspects of talent management, from sourcing to retention assessment to engagement, and development to deployment."[1]

Current Succession Planning Approaches

In researching succession planning strategies currently implemented within organizations, we came to a disturbing discovery. Succession planning is generally not a topic of discussion or planning at a strategic level. Most reports highlight how little planning is being done by organizations. Even in the very sectors that are already facing shortages, like health care, the public service, engineering, and skilled IT, the lack of progress in this HR practice is discouraging. Carson F. Dye in *Healthcare Financial Management* wrote, "Succession planning is as pleasant a topic to discuss as bad breath."[2] *Computerworld* reported that succession planning had not been a top priority for CIOs because of a weak economy and low staff turnover.[3]

Some forward-thinking organizations like General Electric view "succession planning as an integral part of the leadership development process."[4] Not surprisingly, IBM has also been a leader in facing its human resource challenges. They have moved away from the historical replacement model to a "person-focused succession-planning system."[5] Since this organization believes that dynamic market forces require a dynamic workforce, their succession-planning model relies heavily on leaders developing leaders, cross-functional project teams, development on the job, and the IBM competency models and values. These modern mechanisms reflect where IBM is headed—a workforce that is well equipped to solve future business challenges.[6]

Defining Succession Planning

Succession planning is not a new concept. Kings, queens, and politicians, realizing that they were about to retire or die, often had someone waiting in the wings ready to take over the reigns. So, too, is the case in organizations, where CEOs and senior executives often handpick a senior manager that would best fill their shoes and would continue to run the organization in their image.

This system of handpicking potential successors worked well in a business environment that was based upon long-term, unquestioning loyalty and security, a "father knows best" culture. However, such a system doesn't work in today's business climate. Our society has become more ethnically diverse, women continue to make strides both in numbers and positions, and the younger generations have a different set of values and expectations. These groups will not accept a system that they can't influence or in which they can't play an active role. Our workforce today demands that a larger number of people be given an opportunity to reach the managerial or top ranks of an organization. Employees demand a greater democratization of the succession process.

In our knowledge economy, if you don't have the right people to lead your organization, your organization's bottom line will suffer. We have designed a four-point succession planning process to respond to the characteristics and mindset of today's workforce. The four points of our process include the following:

1.   Select the right approach
2.   Analyze your current business state
3.   Analyze your future business state
4.   Execute and evaluate your plan

Point 1: Select the Right Approach

Before HR professionals can even begin to think about creating a succession plan, they must have senior management involvement in selecting the right approach. In selecting the best approach for your organization, senior leaders must balance their own values and expectations with the values and expectations of their workforce. In fact, CEO and senior executive involvement in leadership development (within succession planning) is a "must," not a "nice to have." Eighty-three percent of companies that have high total shareholder return (TSR) have CEOs who are actively involved in supporting and promoting leadership development, compared with 56 percent of companies that have low TSR.[7]

There are three approaches to succession planning: top-down management driven, succession pools, and top-down/ bottom-up. The following chart summarizes each approach. A discussion of the implications of each approach follows, including generational considerations.

Three Succession Planning Approaches

Approach	Characteristics
Top-Down Management Driven	♦ Senior management identifies high-potential employees for succession ♦ Employees may not be told of their "fast track" status ♦ Development plans may be formal but often are informal
Succession Pools	♦ Management task force identifies high potential employees ♦ Employees are told that they are part of a succession-planning process ♦ Development plans are formal
Top-Down/Bottom-Up	♦ Management task force determines competencies and general requirements for succession ♦ Management identifies employees, and employees self-identify (two-way) ♦ Development plans are tailored based on evaluation and performance metrics

Demonstrating Organizational Engagement and Generational Considerations

Top-Down Management Approach

The top-down management driven approach is the least desirable, both from an organizational engagement perspective and from a generational perspective. This approach has difficulty demonstrating any of the three key qualities of engagement: transparency, partnering, and responsiveness. Often, high-potential employees are not informed that they are being secretly groomed for advancement, a contradiction to transparency.

It's not a responsive approach because it doesn't accommodate employees' desires. Management doesn't know whether or not the high-potential employees they have identified are even interested in the future positions. An enormous amount of money might be spent on employees who are not committed to staying with the organization or who have other career interests or who would make a career switch mid-stream in the skill development phase. For example, imagine that you are grooming your manager of sales to become the director or VP of sales in five years, but s/he doesn't know that. S/he tells you two years later that s/he is really interested in operations and has found an organization that will hire her/him at a lower position with growth opportunities in that field. Had you been aware of this employee's career aspirations, you could have invested resources in grooming him/her for a lateral move to operations instead of losing the employee altogether.

The danger of not partnering with employees in succession planning is that they feel a lack of control and autonomy over their careers. When this happens, most will leave an organization. The top-down-management-driven approach doesn't demonstrate partnering because employees are not involved collaboratively in their own development decisions. They feel a limited sense of involvement in the process and accountability for the outcome.

Telecommunications Manufacturer

A global telecommunications hardware manufacturer invites high-potential employees to a two-week leadership training program in the French Alps. These employees are being groomed to be the next generation of leaders but are not told of their status. Also, since attendance is by invitation only, identification of the successors is done exclusively by senior management, with no opportunity for self-identification. The disadvantage of this approach is that it can lead to cloning, subjective selection, and elitism.

Succession Pools Approach

Succession pools rank as a slightly better approach to succession planning. A challenge with this approach is whether or not your organization should inform high-potential employees that they are "in the pool" and managing the negative effects for those employees who aren't selected. For those employees who have made it into the fast track, they may have a sense of entitlement. Entitlement can grow out of being labeled as valuable to the organization. Certainly, it is more transparent if you tell employees that they have been selected and are being groomed for promotion. However, there are risks that need to be managed. It's important for senior leaders to manage the expectations of the employees in the succession pool. Having been selected and receiving development opportunities does *not* guarantee promotion; they simply contribute to an employee's likelihood of progressing in the organization. Managers who can explain "what's in it for them" from an employee perspective (increased skills) and organizational perspective (capacity building and future productivity) will manage overall expectations. By openly communicating the win-win value of being selected, employees are less likely to feel that the organization owes them a promotion.

Those not selected as part of the succession pool, unless they know why, may become disengaged and feel frustrated at not having the opportunity to influence the selection process. The managers/leaders who will identify the succession pool must be prepared to communicate with employees who are not selected why they were excluded and what criteria was used to make their decision. They should provide guidance and direction as to what employees can do, accomplish, improve, or learn in order to be considered next time. Succession pools, unless structured and communicated correctly, contain the danger of not being sufficiently transparent, responsive, or partnering.

Financial Services

A global financial services company constructs action-learning programs for groups of high-potential employees. They receive formal learning, and work on projects relevant to the business. The program is very successful as a learning event and prepares individuals for future positions by refining their business skills. However, it is not clear whether the program results in strong affiliation/commitment and less turn-over.

Top-down/Bottom-up Approach

The top-down/bottom-up is the most desirable approach because it best demonstrates transparency, responsiveness, and partnering. Transparency is demonstrated because this approach is based on a robust performance management system. The objectivity of the performance management system encourages a rational dialogue between managers and employees. Managers discuss with employees the degree to which specific competencies are being demonstrated and how well prepared they are for career advancement.

This approach demonstrates responsiveness because both employees and managers, have access to the criteria and selection process. Because the criteria are openly communicated, managers across the organization are able to respond more effectively and consistently to questions and queries from employees. This approach ensures that subjectivity and/or favoritism are minimized.

A clear performance management and career-pathing process supports and feeds into a top-down/bottom-up approach to succession planning. These systems allow employees to self-assess skill levels and direct their attentions to performance gaps. This encourages partnering and mutual accountability. It may be the case that once employees realize the required competencies for a new role, they will decide to pursue a different position or path. For example, if employees understand exactly what the competencies and expectations are to be a successful people manager in your organization, they may decide that they would rather be a productive individual contributor or a manager of resources rather than people.

U.S. Postal Service[8]

The U.S. Postal Service has recognized the benefits of engaging employees in career and succession planning. During the application stage for a managerial position, employees can either nominate themselves or be nominated by an executive, or officer, for career progression.

From a generational perspective, all four generations want control over their careers. However, the younger generations, in particular, won't tolerate organizational secrecy or managerial subjectivity as it relates to succession planning. Most Traditionalists and Baby Boomers are accustomed to a top-down approach, so for these cohorts, succession pools would be seen as a democratization of the process. If your organization chooses the top-down/bottom-up approach, then Traditionalists and Baby Boomers may need support in evaluating their own developmental needs and career aspirations. These cohorts are used to being told what their gaps are and to being directed as to where and how their careers will develop. They are not accustomed to a collaborative system in which they have negotiating power to express professional desires.

Gen Xers, because of their strong sense of independence and entrepreneurial spirit, respond best to a succession-planning approach in which they have the ability to control the outcome. Gen Xers willingly accept accountability for their career development. They thrive in an environment that encourages them to express, without repercussion, their career goals. Organizations and managers can build trust by encouraging this generation to voice their skill development desires and then create opportunities for them to realize those desires. In order to cultivate that kind of environment, managers need to be strong communicators and collaborators. Today, young employees have greater expectations. They are looking for a better road map for their careers. Many Gen Xers are content to remain within an organization as long as they continue to grow professionally and in the direction of their choice. [9]

Gen Ys, with their high level of social awareness and diversity tolerance, may be offended by a succession-planning approach that encourages cloning and discourages tolerance of diverse thoughts. Because this generation's opinions have always been solicited and valued, it would be completely foreign for Gen Ys to work in an organization that keeps workforce plans a secret. Even succession pools might be problematic for this cohort who may view this approach as unfair because it doesn't allow equal opportunity for everyone. Regardless of which approach you adopt, the criteria for selection must be clear and consistently applied to all employees to engage Gen Y employees successfully.

Point 2: Analyze Your Current Business State

In point 2 of the succession-planning process, a number of factors need identification. First, your organization must identify key roles. In the past, the key roles were only senior management positions—at the C-suite and maybe the senior VP level. With flat organizational hierarchies, middle management plays an increasingly important role from both a functional and management perspective. All management roles need to be evaluated against their impact on the business. Losing a member of a core functional team can also be bad for business. So, individual contributor roles that are critical should be considered for their impact on smooth operations.

There are several sources of data that should be collected to meet the objective of understanding your current business state. First, you need to have a big picture view of your workforce (retirement rates, generational representation, and turnover rates). Second, you need to know why people stay or leave your organization (exit interviews and employee surveys). Third, you need to have a good handle on your industry's labor market conditions (trends and costs). This information helps you to determine whether your strategy should be to go external to recruit talent or whether you should actively develop from within. All of the data collected at this stage of the succession-planning process allows you to have a clear picture of your workforce. You will be able to analyze where you are most at risk, where you have bench strength, and where you need to focus your attention in the short, medium, and long term.

Point 3: Analyze Your Future Business State

HR and senior leaders who undertake succession-planning initiatives must focus on the future as well as the present even though the roles that need to be replaced may not become vacant for another five years. For example, data gathered on your organization's strategy, your industry, and the education environment allows you to create a succession plan that is future oriented. You will know whether or not you need to replace all of the key roles that will be vacated and which new competencies will be required for future business success.

If your business is in a market space that is highly innovative and quickly evolving, then perhaps the IBM methodology that focuses on general leadership and management competencies would best suit your organization's business strategy. If you are uncertain of the jobs/function or roles that you will need five years from now, ensure that your future leaders possess the people and business skills necessary to manage a diverse, changing team.

In analyzing your future business state, it is also important to ask employees what their future plans may be. Many employees will be reluctant to tell you directly that they don't plan to stay with your organization in the future (though Gen Xers and Gen Ys are more inclined to do so). However, many employees will tell you what knowledge and skills they would like to develop. It's not a given that Gen Xers will want the positions soon to be vacated by Baby Boomers.[10] Also, it's important for employees to evaluate whether or not they are interested in remaining a solid contributor or would like to develop into a people manager role. More often than not, organizations promote employees who have functional expertise without assessing whether or not that employee has the ability and/or desire to lead people.

In the past, succession planning was seen as a form of long-range planning. However, given the speed at which the market, technology, and employees' desires change, succession planning must be executed within the scope of short—to medium-range timelines. A robust succession plan should allow for the greatest degree of flexibility and encourage strong cross-functional expertise building as a way of preparing your workforce to excel in the future.

Point 4: Execute and Evaluate Your Plan

To successfully execute your succession plan, a formal implementation framework must be created. Similar to a project plan, the framework should have milestones. These milestones should mark the date of retirement for all key positions and the plan for knowledge transfer. If the role is highly specialized, then the successor needs a longer period to learn the explicit and implicit knowledge of the role. In developing your framework, be sure to engage all appropriate stakeholders. As we mentioned earlier, your senior leaders are key to a successful plan. They are not just key in deciding the right approach, they are also pivotal in the execution of the plan. They need to be involved in the development of people, and they should be champions of the framework within the organization. Other stakeholders that should be involved include employees who will be retiring, managers, and employees (in particular, if you adopt a top-down-management-driven approach).

Your framework must be dynamic and able to fluctuate with both consumer and labor market trends, requiring continuous calibration. With the support of robust learning and development and performance management systems, both managers and employees alike can identify desired career paths, competencies, and learning paths required to achieve organizational and employee goals. HR's role is to manage the implementation of the framework by partnering with both leaders and the front line to identify positions, assess potential employees, and monitor the execution of the promotion/lateral move plan.[11]

Metrics that matter

Some examples of quantitative metrics you can use to evaluate your succession plan on an ongoing basis include the following:

- Retention rates for high-potential employees
- Management involvement in developing their people (coaching, mentoring, etc.)
- Number of employees who self-identify they would like to be promoted
- Number of promotions/lateral moves based on development plans
- Number of key roles filled by internal versus external resources
- Training investment in developing high-potential employees
- Performance success of employees after promotion
- Transfer of knowledge from upcoming retirees to new employees

Sample Engagement Survey—Succession Planning

Transparency demonstrated by specific, accurate, and open communication

- ☐ Do employees understand your organization's succession-planning approach and its intended business outcome?
- ☐ Can employees access detailed role descriptions with related competencies and learning paths?
- ☐ Are promotions and job gaps openly communicated and open for competition across the organization?

Responsiveness demonstrated by timeliness and feedback

- ☐ Does your organization have a clear process, or mechanism, to allow employees to switch departments, roles, or functions?
- ☐ Do employees have control over the speed of their succession?
- ☐ Is your succession plan reviewed and updated regularly with input from multiple levels?

Partnering demonstrated by the organization / managers collaborating with their employees

- ☐ Do employees have individualized development plans that balance organizational goals and personal goals?
- ☐ Do your managers regularly hold meetings with direct reports to discuss career interests?
- ☐ Does your organization encourage employees to think about opportunities outside of their functional area or role?

* *While these questions are based on a yes/no response, a Likert scale may provide richer data, depending on the size and complexity of your organization. Be sure to analyze data along demographic lines as well.*

Chapter Twelve

Management Practices: Engage Me as an Investor Don't Demotivate Me

It has been noted throughout various sections of this book the importance that managers and leaders play in getting, keeping, and growing talent. The top reason that employees leave an organization is their relationship with their direct manager.[1] So your organization can't afford to have bad managers. The turnover costs and decline in employee engagement resulting from bad managers far outweighs any functional expertise they bring to a team. Regardless of age, all employees seek a positive and collaborative relationship with their manager. However, the grace period that Gen X or Gen Y employees give managers to get the relationship right is much shorter than that of Baby Boomers or Traditionalists. For this reason, managers should be trained, supported, and skilled in creating a work environment that motivates and engages all four generations. In managing employees, managers must be able to create a work environment that is characterized by the following:[2]

- Is relatively autonomous
- Celebrates achievements
- Creates a sense of purpose, direction, and excitement about achieving organizational goals

❧ Provides challenging/fulfilling work

❧ Enables employees to gain new skills

❧ Provides top management support

To create a workplace culture that inspires employee engagement—characterized by expenditure of discretionary effort, emotional connection to your organization, and acceptance of accountability—managers must focus on three broad areas:

1. Communication

2. Collaboration

3. Coaching

Communication

Strong managers and leaders provide frequent, timely, and relevant communication to their teams. They create a two-way dialogue with employees by soliciting ideas and feedback from employees who want to participate in decision making. Creating a top-down/bottom-up approach to communication allows managers to stay in touch with the pulse of their teams. They are able to proactively identify engagement issues and respond to them before employees leave the organization or become disengaged. Being an effective communicator requires a focus on the following:

❧ Being proactive

❧ Being clear

❧ Being consistent

Proactive communication provides employees with information well in advance, allowing them time to internalize how the content impacts their roles. It sets a positive stage for organizational or team changes by allowing employees the opportunity to ask questions and communicate comments prior to implementation. Proactive communication also enables you to begin the process of repetitively communicating your message. A message needs to be communicated several times before it is internalized. By proactively communicating, you will increase the likelihood of your message being heard, understood, and executed upon. Being clear in your communication requires that employees have enough information to fully understand your intended message—not just high-level information, but all of the details. Ask yourself, Will my team members understand why we are doing this? Will they know what actions to take? If not, rework your communication to ensure that sufficient details are provided to explain the objective of your communication and your expected outcome and action steps. Consistent communication means that you communicate the same message over time. It also requires that your communication be congruent with other messages you have communicated in the past.

Our Six Step Communication Plan program provides managers with a simple process for being proactive, clear, and consistent in their communication. Managers are required to craft their messages in advance, incorporating knowledge of generational preferences regarding key messages, medium, and frequency. It also requires that managers solicit feedback from their target audience and commit to following up. Following a consistent process becomes increasingly important when communicating organizational, departmental, or individual role changes.

Aon Reed Stenhouse Inc.

Our communication workshop was rolled out to managers at Aon Reed Stenhouse Inc. with the objectives of providing a clear, simple process for communication and increasing employee engagement/action. Managers were provided with a six step communication plan, which they completed as part of an action-learning assignment. Each manager crafted a communication plan for the announcement of a departmental/team change and delivered his/her message to a multigenerational audience. Coaching and feedback was provided by team members, colleagues, and ourselves through a debrief of each assignment.

Demonstrating Organizational Engagement and Generational Considerations

Each generation has different expectations of the frequency and transparency of communication. Traditionalists have been accustomed to a work world where communication was delivered top-down; their opinions were rarely solicited, and information was provided on a need-to-know basis. For this reason, formal communication is expected only quarterly or annually from senior leaders. You engage Traditionalists by being transparent about how your message links to corporate goals and objectives. The communication provides a direct link to how the organization will benefit operationally and the impact it will have on Traditionalists building their legacy.

Baby Boomers have experienced a lot of corporate changes that were initially communicated as great for the organization but turned out to be bad for them. By being transparent and open, you build trust with this cohort. They are cautious of how your message impacts them and their ability to add value to the organization/team. Baby Boomers desire open communication where they can share their feelings, opinions, and suggestions. Demonstrate partnering with Baby Boomers by communicating in a style that focuses on consensus building and gaining commitment.

For Gen Xers, they have an expectation that your communication style is a two-way dialogue. This cohort desires frequent communication, on a weekly basis, focused on achieving results. Being transparent in your communication is particularly important when communicating to Gen Xers given their skepticism of managerial motives. This cohort won't just accept your message because you're a senior manager or leader. They want to understand all of the details and motives behind the message. By partnering with this cohort to solicit feedback from them, you engage and motivate them to participate in decisions that impact team and individual performance results.

Gen Ys have a strong expectation that your communication be partnering and responsive. They expect you to solicit their input and act upon their suggestions. Also, given this cohort's sense of fair play, just-in-time communication about your actions and decisions gains their trust. This generation desires frequent, perhaps daily, communication with managers. They have an expectation that they can share ideas, thoughts, and questions with you 24/7, via technology. Because Gen Ys have such a fluid work style, the speed at which you communicate and respond to them determines how responsive and partnering they believe you are. Establishing communication protocols regarding your response times and access is important in managing Gen Y's expectations.

Collaboration

Managers set the foundation for cultivating a collaborative team environment by communicating effectively with employees. As a manager, your role in creating a collaborative team environment is critical. It's important to understand how to create a high-performance team by demonstrating core competencies such as communication, decision-making, and interpersonal skills and elite competencies such as innovation, strategic thinking, and leading change. We define a high-performance team as

> A small group of highly effective and cohesive individuals with complimentary skills who are equally committed to a common purpose, goal and work approach for which they hold themselves mutually accountable.[3]

At a manager level, there are observable behaviors that you should demonstrate in order to support and encourage a collaborative, high-performance team. At an employee level, team members must also commit to demonstrating specific behaviors that cultivate a positive working environment. Strong managers focus on negotiation and influencing skills as a foundation for successful collaboration. They establish a conflict-resolution process so as to minimize team conflict, employing a collaborative problem-solving approach when it does occur.

Our Building a High Performance Team program works with managers and team members to evaluate their current performance as it relates to seven core competencies and eight elite competencies. Each competency is defined with associated performance outcomes and observable behaviors for the leaders and team members.

Global IT Manufacturer

At a global IT manufacturer of hardware and software, we worked with an internal team to identify areas of strength and areas of opportunity in order to achieve greater team performance. While the team was highly competent, often exceeding performance targets, they recognized the need to improve some of the core and elite competencies to reach the next level of performance. Our role was to rank both the team's performance as well as the leader's performance against the competencies. Once the performance analysis was complete, we conducted a team workshop to explore the impact of the results; discuss individual, team, and leader accountabilities; and develop action plans.

Demonstrating Organizational Engagement and Generational Considerations

Collaboration, by definition, requires that you take a partnering and responsive approach when working with your team. Creating a collaborative environment also requires that you create awareness and understanding among team members of generational differences and potential clash points. As discussed in chapter 2, generational differences in work styles can cause dysfunction within teams, particularly as this relates to responding to conflict. Your role is to ensure that all four generations work collaboratively together to exceed performance standards. This objective is achieved by being transparent about differences among the team members and communicating how best to maximize each generation's strengths.

Traditionalists appreciate a collaborative work culture that values their experience and allows them to partner with younger colleagues to share past experiences. This cohort may struggle with a team environment where decision making isn't centralized. Baby Boomers seek a collaborative approach, one that ensures everyone has an opportunity to participate in group discussions and decision making. This generation may struggle with younger colleagues who want less face-to-face collaboration and more interaction via technology. For Gen Xers, collaboration around work schedule and workload is most important as this allows them to maintain a strong work-life balance. This cohort may clash with colleagues who perceive team collaboration as team consensus and group work, not individual actions that contribute to team results. Gen Ys seek a collaborative team environment, using technology to stay connected. They want opportunities to provide input, feedback, and opinions. This generation may struggle with the need to have face-to-face team meetings and adhere to strict communication protocols based on level of authority. By focusing on the strengths that each generation brings to the team, you can create an environment of respect and recognition of the value of all team members.

Coaching

Managers who have the right skills and the desire to coach their employees contribute to the success of your people strategy. Effective coaching is a relationship between a coach and a coachee. The relationship empowers the coachee to focus on improving identified skills and develop new behaviors.[4] Coaching is a unique event, outside of performance management, that is designed to unlock human potential. The objective is to create a work environment that is conducive to helping employees reach their full potential. There are four types of coaching conversations you can have with employees, and they are the following:

1. Positive performance results—analyze achieved successes
2. Job-task progression—identify progress and improvements
3. Innovation and creativity—analyze creative and innovative results
4. Performance gap identification—identify skills and behaviors that require improvement

Regardless of which type of coaching conversation you are having, to be a great coach, you need to establish a strong collaborative relationship with employees and demonstrate a commitment to open, two-way communication. Effective coaching is characterized by the following competencies:

- ✓ Specific
- ✓ Timely
- ✓ Action Orientated
- ✓ Results Focused
- ✓ Transparent

Our START coaching program provides managers with the tools to tap into the motivations and expectations of all four generations by creating a collaborative coaching environment that addresses the Traditionalists' preference for structure, the Baby Boomers' desire for balanced feedback, the Gen Xers' need for specific and objective feedback, and the Gen Ys' desire for transparent, two-way coaching.

Mutual Fund Company

Our START Coaching program was delivered at a North American mutual fund company. The objective was to increase managers' coaching abilities and create an environment of greater collaboration and empowerment. The first step in our process was to assess managers' current coaching abilities against our coaching model by collecting feedback from their employees. Next, we created individualized coaching assignments based on each manager's area of need, providing them with a report of his/her initial evaluation. Managers then attended our workshop, which focused on layering on a generational perspective to coaching and motivation. Following the program, each manager completed two coaching events over a six-week period. After each coaching event, their employee (coachee) rated their performance. A final report was provided indicating areas of improvement and areas of continued opportunity. An overall team rating was compiled and senior leaders were given tips on how to "coach the coach" and how to create a culture of coaching on an ongoing basis.

Demonstrating Organizational Engagement and Generational Considerations

Your coaching approach and process should be aligned to generational motivations and expectations. Similar to performance discussions and mentoring, Traditionalists have not had a lot of exposure to collaborative coaching conversations. Members of this generation may need assistance in self-identifying skills that require coaching and the type of coaching assignments that will work best for them. Traditionalists need to be reassured that coaching is an ongoing process designed to help them improve, not monitor or keep track of their wins and losses. Transparency around your coaching motives and intentions is important in making Traditionalists feel comfortable with the process.

Baby Boomers also have not experienced a lot of direct coaching. As we shifted to a competency-based work culture, coaching has become a more common practice.

However, many Boomers are often uncomfortable giving and receiving coaching. A partnering approach to coaching—meaning, employees self-reflecting on their own areas of strength and development—helps Baby Boomers to become more engaged in the process. It highlights their wins while also identifying areas for development in a non-threatening way.

Gen Xers are eager to receive coaching since it provides them with an opportunity to develop new skills that they feel are marketable and aligned to their career aspirations. In particular, performance gap coaching for this cohort should be specific and timely. It's of little use to Gen Xers to receive coaching on an area of development several months after they complete a project. Members of this cohort want to know right away exactly how they can improve so that they can achieve greater results immediately. This cohort will also challenge you to be specific about the coaching you provide. Making motherhood statements such as "You need to be more strategic" may result in a Gen Xer not buying into your assessment and disengaging. Given this generation's openness to providing direct feedback to their managers, you can easily partner with them. Solicit feedback on your coaching/management abilities and collaboratively identify ways to better connect and engage with Gen X employees.

Gen Ys also seek similar coaching experiences as Gen Xers but may require even more frequent access to you. Members of this cohort are eager to learn how they can contribute to the team's success yet may require a lot of direction to ensure they are improving their skills or demonstrating the right behaviors. Many in this cohort have been unaccustomed to receiving coaching or feedback that is negative in any way. Therefore, you should take a partnering approach when providing coaching on performance gaps. Allow Gen Ys to self-identify how they can improve prior to providing them with coaching direction. Being transparent about your coaching process and objectives helps Gen Ys understand the desired outcome—improved performance. Focusing on the objective makes this cohort feel more at ease with receiving coaching that is focused on areas of development, not just areas of strength.

Metrics That Matter

Some examples of quantitative metrics you can use to evaluate your management practices are the following:

- ❧ Manager assessments—360-degree assessments
- ❧ Retention/turnover rates by manager/team/department
- ❧ Engagement scores by manager/team/department
- ❧ Frequency of communication by manager/team/department
- ❧ Frequency of coaching conversations
- ❧ Employee assessment of workplace culture—factors that impact engagement and motivation
- ❧ Team performance inventory

Sample Engagement Survey—Management Practices

Transparency demonstrated by specific, accurate, and open communication

- ☐ Do managers communicate their intentions and objectives on a regular basis?
- ☐ Do employees understand their role and their manager's role in providing coaching?
- ☐ Are managers and employees clear about what competencies/observable behaviors must be demonstrated to be a high-performance team?

Responsiveness demonstrated by timeliness and feedback

- ☐ Do managers solicit, listen to, and respond to employee feedback and suggestions on their performance?
- ☐ Are managers skilled at managing expectations through negotiation and influencing?
- ☐ Do managers provide coaching that is frequent and specific enough for all employee groups?

Partnering demonstrated by the organization/managers collaborating with employees

- ☐ Do managers create a two-way dialogue with employees?
- ☐ Do managers increase team performance through greater awareness of differences?
- ☐ Do coaching conversations allow employees to self identify areas of development?

* *While these questions are based on a yes/no response, a Likert scale may provide richer data, depending on the size and complexity of your organization. Be sure to analyze data along demographic lines as well.*

Conclusion

In this book, we had an ambitious undertaking. We described elements and components that current people strategies need to consider, including how these strategies can demonstrate organizational engagement. More importantly, we revealed how these people strategies would be successful in targeting all four generations in the workplace. The discussions, techniques, and strategies help to maximize the human capital of today and tomorrow. The question remains, what else does the future hold?

Organizations will always struggle to get, keep, and grow talent. They will continue to face internal and external forces that could derail their ability to acquire, manage, value, and invest in human capital. In this conclusion, we highlight internal and external forces that organizations need to keep their eyes on. At this point, we only provide a brief overview of the issues as we will continue to study their impact on people strategies in the future.

Recession: What happens if North America experiences a recession in the next few years?

Even if we face a recession again, as we did in the mid-'80s and early '90s, we don't believe that the impact on the labor market will be as severe as it was then. The reason is that thousands of Baby Boomers are retiring each day. So while the demand-side labor market may become smaller, it won't flip to a supply-side anytime soon. More importantly, the manager/leadership cadre will be drawn from the Gen X cohort, which is much smaller than the Baby Boomer cohort. Certain sectors, in particular the public sector, will struggle to retain Baby Boomers because of current pension plans. Baby Boomers that remain in the workforce will do so in different roles and capacities.

Also, more and more women are entering into the workforce past the age of forty-five. With increased female participation and an aging workforce, organizations will need to be careful not to focus too heavily on any one employee market. They can't alienate the experienced worker in favor of the younger worker or vice versa.

Unions: What is the impact of the generational identities on union membership?

There is some indication that unions struggle with growing their membership within the Gen X and Gen Y ranks. Most unions are built on Traditionalist values, where seniority, tenure, and obedience to the collective are the founding principles. This model is incongruous with Gen Xers' desires for independence and merit-based performance rewards. It does align with Gen Ys value of respecting the collective but is contradictory to their desire for fairness based on principles of competence. For some organizations, there may be a greater opportunity to work collaboratively with unions as the next generation of union leaders will look to negotiate using different guiding principles.

Technology: What will increasing technological capabilities mean for the way we work?

We anticipate that the restructuring of how and where we do work will only increase. Gen Ys in particular will insist that not only the workday, but also work styles, be changed. They will redefine the process of collaboration through technology. However, organizations will have to be careful not to let technology become the solution, but rather a tool in achieving performance goals. Leaders will have to work diligently to identify the best ways to do business, even when people rarely meet face-to-face. Client-facing departments will need to balance how to service clients while meeting the expectations of employees to work in new ways.

Globalization/Immigration: What will be the impact of globalization and immigration on our workplaces?

Globalization implies the broadening of reach to increasing foreign markets. New operational frameworks will be created that will encourage high levels of productivity. The average employee will need to learn different skill sets to work transnationally without ever leaving his/her region. When you can't meet face-to-face and are only working over e-mail or phone, interpersonal skills become even more important. Also, given our shrinking labor pool, many organizations are now welcoming more immigrant employees. Governments will have to work with and perhaps put pressure on professional organizations to increase the speed and to recognize foreign workers' qualifications. Organizations who want to maintain a competitive advantage will view the influx of diverse thoughts from foreign employees as an opportunity to be more creative and innovative. The way to ensure continued operational productivity will be to create frameworks in which diverse thought and work approaches are truly merged, not just tolerated by the existing dominant approach.

Offshoring: Is it the answer?

While offshoring might be a solution for many back-office functions, we continue to witness the struggle that organizations have when they offshore client-facing functions. Many organizations, for both brand image and productivity reasons, have reclaimed those front-office functions. Some organizations have created a hybrid model in which they have service centers both locally and abroad. The success of these initiatives lies with consumer perceptions. As always, the consumer decides if operational decisions meet their needs. For continued success, it's critical to deliver seamless service. However, we are facing a shrinking labor pool so consumers may be forced to accept new standards of service.

Mindset: Will the employee mindset of the future remain the same?

Given the pedagogy and parental influences that Gen Ys are exposed to, we see an increasing actualization of the employee mindset we described in chapter 1. The pedagogy is becoming more and more personalized to students, with the objective of building self-esteem and helping every student graduate. These students (your future workforce) know when they're doing a good job and when they're not. However, often, they are being rewarded without demonstrating high levels of performance. In part, the challenge is that effort is being rewarded, rather than results. This is causing students and employees to quit tasks if they don't succeed the first time. For organizations, this will demand an intensive focus on connecting, facilitating, and creating strategies that ensure a smooth transfer for new employees into the workplace.

Career definition: How will careers be defined?

A successful career will no longer be defined by an organization or even an industry. As employees increasingly switch organizations, industries, and careers, success will be defined by levels of contribution. Increasingly, Gen X and Gen Y employees move in and out of the workforce to look for meaning in other parts of their lives (relationships, travel, and volunteering). This new reality of a transient, "serial retiree" workforce will require organizations to reevaluate the structure and timing of career paths, job structure, how people and projects are managed, and entry to and exit from organizational processes.

HR: What is the future role of HR departments?

HR will focus exclusively on servicing employees through creating systems and frameworks that become decentralized in their day-to-day execution. To do so, HR leaders will need to determine guiding principles out of which these systems and frameworks are built. HR will have a permanent seat at the C-suite table as there will be no successful business plan unless there is a concurrent people plan. This will trickle down throughout the organization as HR generalists will collaborate with operations to construct execution plans that will be tied to achieving business results.

HR will have to accept increasing accountability for the success of key performance indicators on the organization's scorecard if they wish to be a strategic partner. Operational performance success cannot be solely the responsibility of the business units. To become partners with line managers, HR must demonstrate how they will help managers to translate people strategies and programs into day-to-day action. An increasing partnership or shared accountability structure will be created in which operations cannot proceed without HR's involvement. Conversely, HR cannot create frameworks and strategies unless they have analyzed and designed them to be successful within operational environments.

In the future, there will be challenges and opportunities in creating high-performance, people-focused organizations. Internal factors such as the new employee mindset, the changing role of unions, and new career definitions will force organizations to change. The work environment will change to one that is flexible yet focused on superior performance results. The external forces such as economic fluctuations, increasing global expansion, offshoring, and technological advances will force organizations to be nimble in their response to remain competitive. Organizations will maximize their existing human capital while investing in new, innovative ways to do business. The C-suite, in partnership with human resource leaders, must lead the charge. Your role will be to proactively create systems and frameworks that are responsive to business needs and push the boundaries of your organizational structures and culture.

Appendix

Four Generations—Four Approaches to Work and Life

Given that employees hold a greater bargaining chip, there is an increasing need for organizations to create an engaged relationship with all employee groups. To get, keep, and grow the best employees, it is critical to understand your employee markets: who they are, what they want and expect from your organization, and how they differ from one another.

Today's workplace is comprised of four generations:

Traditionalists	1922-1945
Baby Boomers	1946-1964
Gen Xers	1965-1980
Gen Ys	1981-2000

Generational cohorts possess unique values, characteristics, and skills based on their experiences of life-defining events. The commonality of experiences creates generational identities. The generational identities are the viewpoints that each cohort has on life, love, family, work, politics, and society. These characteristics are important to understand because they impact individual, team, and organizational performance. This appendix describes the characteristics, life-defining events, and values of each generation.

Traditionalists as the Brick Builders of Corporate North American Culture

Traditionalists		
Life-defining Events	Attitudes, Values, and Expectations	Key Characteristics
◆ The Great Depression	◆ Loyalty	◆ Compliant
◆ World War II	◆ Respect for authority	◆ Stable
◆ Peal Harbor	◆ Dedication	◆ Detail-orientated
◆ Korean War	◆ Sacrifice	◆ Hardworking
◆ Golden age of radio	◆ Conformity	◆ Dedicated
◆ Emergence of the silver screen	◆ Honor	◆ Fiscally frugal
	◆ Privacy	◆ Trustworthy
◆ Rise of labor unions	◆ Stability	◆ Risk averse
	◆ Economic conservatism	◆ Long-term focused

The oldest generation in the workforce is the Traditionalists, also referred to as Veterans or the Silent Generation. This cohort was born between1922 and 1945 and grew up in a time of world wars and post-war rebuilding. Many Traditionalists, whose urban parents were devastated by the stock market crash of 1929, grew up during the Depression Era. It was a time when people learned to do without. Creativity was required to make even the smallest amounts of food, clothing, and money stretch even further.

The hardship of the wars and the Great Depression greatly affected this generation's values and opinions toward family, religion, work, and government. Members of this cohort lived in nuclear families that were patriotic and supportive of the government. They attended formal religious services and learned right from wrong in schools. Respect for authority and adherence to the rules were enforced using corporal punishment. Traditionalists learned that working hard and playing by the rules were the ways to success. The Traditionalists transferred these values of dedication, loyalty, honor, and sacrifice to the workplace, where they are often described as hardworking, possessing a strong work ethic, and compliant with organizational policies and practices.

The Organization Man, written by William Whyte in the mid-1950s, defined the Traditionalist era in terms of job security and stability.[1] It also described the expectations of what a good job should be. During this time, Traditionalists were socialized to believe that if they worked hard, paid their dues, and were loyal to a company, they would receive a decent wage, lifetime employment, and a pension when they retired. Employees didn't job hop; they were with their organization for life.[2] To be successful, employees dedicated themselves to their organizations and committed themselves with the same gusto as they did to their spouses. The workday was predictable, and work was completed in a linear fashion. Succession plans were clear and straightforward. Employees knew what their next job would be and how long it would take them to climb the corporate ladder. To be a true "organization man," you were likely a white North American male who could easily fit into the corporate culture. This meant dressing, acting, and speaking like your superiors and colleagues.

From a leadership perspective, managers used a command-and-control style to manage their staff. Title, role, and seniority dictated the level of respect managers received. A larger office with a view and nicer furniture and carpeting were status symbols within the workplace. Senior executives were served meals on fine china and had their own private bathrooms. The corporate culture promoted a divide between management and employees or workers. Often, there was an "us and them" mentality in many organizations—meaning, employees of different rank and status didn't socialize together.

Many characteristics of this type of organizational culture don't exist today, having been largely changed by existing Baby Boomer leaders. However, the Traditionalists' values and expectations have shaped corporate America and are still evident in many large, formal institutions such as banks, insurance companies, and federal departments/agencies. This cohort's goal is to build and leave a legacy in both social and organizational endeavors. Traditionalists like to work on projects and assignments that allow them to make a lasting contribution to your organizations' success. Being the creators of the brick-and-mortar world, they want to ensure that something concrete and real is left behind for the next generation even after they have retired.

Profile of a Traditionalist

William is a sixty-two-year-old "company man" with a large packaged-goods company. He has worked his entire career in the finance department. He is an accountant by trade but is missing the accreditation of being a certified accountant because he did not have the opportunity to go to university. As a young man at nineteen years old, he began working for the company as a bookkeeper. He married a year later, and his wife, Laura, gave birth to two sons within the first three years of marriage. Laura was a stay-at-home mother, caring for their children, managing the household, and supporting William in his career. Over the years, as William was promoted and made more money, the family benefited by taking vacations together in their station wagon. In his 40s, William focused on helping his sons pay for their education. It was important to him that his children have opportunities he never had.

By his mid-50s, William was earning enough money to afford a nicer car and a larger house, but instead, he chose to save his money for retirement. He was looking forward to spending time with his grandchildren. As an employee, William is described by his colleagues, direct reports, and his manager as a hardworking, dependable, and honest person. He is proud of his attendance record, having only missed twenty days in over forty years of work, including the extra few days he took off after the birth of his sons. He likes the people he works with but doesn't socialize with them outside the office. Over the years, he has attended every Christmas party and family summer barbeque the company has hosted.

Now in his early 60s, William is looking forward to retirement next year. Since he has always paid into the company pension plan and put a little extra money aside, he and Laura can enjoy a comfortable retirement with little concern. As their forty-fifth wedding anniversary approaches, he looks forward to taking Laura on their first overseas vacation to see parts of the world they have always dreamed of visiting.

Home Depot[3]

Home Depot has actively targeted the Traditionalists generation for employment in their stores, as a way of fulfilling their commitment to customers to provide knowledgeable, helpful, and engaged associates. By leveraging the experience and expertise of Traditionalists who have worked in carpentry, flooring, and millwork before, these employees are well positioned to improve customer service and help coach younger, less-experienced colleagues.

Baby Boomers as the Rebellious Generation That Was Forced to Conform

Baby Boomers		
Life-defining Events	Attitudes, Values, and Expectations	Key Characteristics
◆ Civil rights movement	◆ Optimism	◆ Driven to succeed
◆ Women's liberation	◆ Involvement	◆ Team players
◆ Cuban missile crisis	◆ Team-orientated	◆ Relationship-focused
◆ Vietnam war	◆ Personal growth and gratification	◆ Eager to add value
◆ Quebec crisis and Bill 101	◆ Youthfulness	◆ Politically savvy in the workplace
◆ Trudeau era—multiculturalism	◆ Equality	◆ Competitive
◆ The cold war	◆ Career-focused	
◆ Woodstock		
◆ Neil Armstrong landing on the moon		
◆ Television as the dominant media		

The Baby Boomers were born between 1946 and 1964.[4] As children of traditionalist parents, Boomers enjoyed a child-focused upbringing. They were wanted by their parents who focused on them and raised them in a new era of possibilities. As children, Boomers grew up in optimistic, positive times. The economy was booming after the war, and this period had the highest fertility rates in almost two hundred years.[5] They were doted on by parents, teachers, and their communities. Similar to the social trend of nesting after 9/11, the '60s was an era of idealism around family life and social responsibility. With over 87 million Boomers across North America, the sheer size of this generation influenced the expansion of suburbs, hospitals, and schools. Boomers grew accustomed to being in the spotlight and learned that because there were so many of them, they could influence traditional systems to accommodate their needs.

Boomers entered adulthood with anti-authoritarian attitudes. Intent on redefining social and political institutions, they adopted and pushed forward many of the social causes their parents had started, such as the civil rights and gender equality movements. The problem was that this demographic power, which worked in their favor at rallies, marches, and on voting days, worked against them in the workplace. Since there were so many of them, employment was controlled by supply and demand. If a boomer employee didn't want to follow the rules, there were ten other people lined up outside to take his/her job. This high degree of competition caused many Boomers to reassess their commitment to challenging the status quo. Some in this cohort willingly conceded to the corporate world built on Traditionalist values, while others were forced to conform out of necessity. Either way, this generation experienced a general mellowing of their rebellious characteristics.

Boomers adapted to the competition and made it their own. Well-known for their workaholic tendencies, members of this generation brought in fifty-, sixty—or seventy-hour work weeks in many industries. They coined the term "Thank God it's Monday" and threw themselves whole-heartedly into their careers. The workplace became highly political. Colleagues who, on the surface, appeared to be collaborative and supportive of each other were in reality each vying for the attention of the management. They needed to be politically savvy and to work hard in order to distinguish themselves from their colleagues. They worked hard to demonstrate how they added value to an organization, thereby differentiating themselves from the competition. Boomers' careers became their symbol of value and self-worth. Often, the drive toward professional goals, achievement, and promotions were at the expense of family and social activities. This generation tends to live to work rather than work to live.

Unlike their predecessors, Boomers adopted new characteristics mid-career. The impact of corporate downsizing and massive layoffs in the late '80s and early '90s had a profound effect on this cohort's identity. They had entered the work environment with an expectation of loyalty and stability, similar to Traditionalists. Most in this cohort had made personal sacrifices to build their careers. When Boomers experienced downsizing, their mindset toward work changed.[6] They realized that years of experience and expertise were no guarantee of continued employment. Many Boomers found themselves, for the first time in their lives, without a sense of purpose and identity. Up until that point, their careers had been their identity. They were emotionally devastated in losing their jobs, realizing that their employers' loyalty to them and cradle-to-grave job security were gone. Many were financially devastated by downsizing because they had no money in reserve to carry them over while they looked for another job. In the aftermath of downsizing, the new focus for many Boomers was to have a work-life balance. A balance that would allow this cohort to gain satisfaction from their careers while also focusing time and energy on their families, friends, and themselves.

As a cohort, this generation seems to evolve more than Traditionalists and Gen Xers. From anti-authoritarian college students to corporate yuppies to health and fitness focused parents—Boomers continuously define and redefine who they are. Today, as Boomers face middle age, they are redefining historical notions of age, youth, and beauty. However, the core traits of Boomers such as adding value in whatever they do, being politically savvy and competitive in their careers remain the same.

As the largest generation, Boomers continue to shape our political, social, and organizational landscapes. Politically, Boomers demand more from government, such as increased social security and expanded Medicare programs. Due to their buying power, this generation's expectations are addressed in the marketplace, be it retirement planning, leisure activities, or medical innovations. From employers, Boomers demand organizational policies and practices that support them in balancing family obligations and challenging careers. Since many in this cohort are caring for both aging parents and young children, they seek HR programs and policies that allow them to manage their dual role as parent and caregiver. This cohort's goal is to put their stamp on things; therefore, they seek opportunities and experiences that allow them to add value to an organization and contribute in a way that secures their position.

Profile of a Baby Boomer

Jane is a forty-four-year-old divorcee with two children. Up until four years ago, Jane had always worked in sales with a blue-chip company. She was employed with the organization for fifteen years. Jane was aggressive and confident enough to land big accounts, and as a result, became increasingly more successful in the 80s and 90s. While her colleagues struggled to acquire new customers, Jane relied on her large rolodex of business contacts. She always believed in the value of networking; she learnt early in her career that it was not *what* she knew but *who* she knew that would make her successful. After a downturn in the economy, she was let go from her employer with little severance and barely a "thank you" from the department that she had helped grow. After being laid off, Jane went back to school to learn new skills in public relations.

She currently works for a midsize financial services firm as a public relations specialist. She is able to leverage her knowledge of finance within her new role. She was required to take a step back in her career from a salary standpoint because her product knowledge was limited. When she looked for a job, no one offered her a pay level reflective of her twenty-plus years of experience, especially since she was starting in a new role. She reports to a manager who is ten years younger than her. Jane is upset to find out that some of her colleagues make more money than she does.

Jane's daughter is in high school and her son is in elementary school. While she can't stay at home with them, Jane is committed to her children. Her weekends are spent chauffeuring her son to hockey games and her daughter to the mall. Jane often takes work home at night but tries to leave the office early enough so she can have dinner with her kids at least a few nights a week. Dinner often consists of take-out food in front of the TV after 7 p.m., because everyone has such a busy schedule. Jane is pleased with her new career and is hopeful that she can establish the same level of success she did in sales. But she is cautious not to put too much of herself on the line. Her trust of organizations and managers has weakened but has not been totally destroyed. She believes that if she works hard and aligns herself with the right people, she will succeed again.

The Liquor Control Board of Ontario (LCBO)

The LCBO is a provincial government enterprise and a large retailer with some 600 stores in the province. With a majority of its workforce being Baby Boomers (55 percent), the LCBO recognized the need to help managers understand the impact generational differences may have on team performance, employee and customer engagement, and retention of younger employees. As the LCBO makes a shift from a Traditionalist structure to a more open, collaborative, and transparent culture, Baby Boomer managers have been well equipped to manage the employee of the future by using a variety of leadership tools and techniques that motivate and engage all four generations.

Gen Xers as the Slackers Who Grew Up Quickly

Gen Xers		
Life-defining Events	Attitudes, Values, and Expectations	Key Characteristics
◆ Much Music/MTV	◆ Independence	◆ Techno-literate
◆ Personal computers	◆ Self-reliance	◆ Flexible and adaptable
◆ AIDS	◆ Pragmatism	◆ Creative
◆ The Challenger disaster	◆ Skepticism	◆ Entrepreneurial
◆ Massive corporate downsizing	◆ Informality	◆ Multi-tasker
◆ Regan/Mulroney conservatism	◆ Balance	◆ Results-driven
◆ Fall of Berlin Wall		◆ Individualistic
◆ Operation Dessert Storm		
◆ Los Angeles riots		
◆ The Canadian Charter of Rights and Freedoms		
◆ Quebec separation referendum		

Gen X is the smaller cohort that followed the baby boom. Those born in this generation (1965-1980) are often referred to as baby busters or twentysomethings. Gen X has been labeled the "lost" generation. Living in the shadow of the boom, this generation did not get the same level of attention by the media, the marketers, or the government as Boomers did. Many born in this cohort don't like the label Gen X because it is associated with negative characteristics such as being slackers who lack the strong work ethic and dedication of their predecessors.

Members of this generation grew up in one of the most anti-child decades.[7] They were the first children to be born to women who took pills to prevent them; more children from this generation than ever before were born to single mothers. Between 1991 and 1996, one-parent families increased in Canada by 83,000 representing over 1.1 million, the largest majority at 945,000 being led by single mothers.[8]

Divorce and dual-income families resulted in latchkey kids who needed to assume responsibility for taking care of themselves. When they came home after school, they fixed their own snack, sat down alone to do their homework, and waited for their parent(s) to come home. This focus on independence at an early age is a cornerstone of the Gen X identity. This cohort learned to take responsibility for their own lives early on.

Gen Xers came of age during a time when the labor market shifted from one of commitment and loyalty to a single employer over a long-term career to one in which employees had to adapt within an insecure workplace environment.[9] As they watched the economic turbulence of the '80s, Gen Xers developed a strong sense of guardedness and cynicism about the future. Gen Xers experienced frustration because of limited employment and educational opportunities and a generally weak overall economy.[10] University and college enrolments that had been increased to accommodate the Boomers shrunk in the '80s and '90s because there was a surplus of graduates in the labor market. The Gen Xers who did attend postsecondary education found that upon graduation, they couldn't find meaningful employment. They were now competing with the downsized Baby Boomers for entry-level positions.

The need to control their own destiny was reinforced to Gen Xers as they witnessed their parents or their parents' friends fall victim to corporate downsizing. Their families were impacted by the financial, social, and psychological effects of unemployment. While many Boomers were forced to confront the new organizational and employment reality mid career, Gen Xers never experienced it any other way. They entered the work environment with no expectation of a long-term career path with a single organization or of receiving loyalty from an employer.

Many Gen Xers vowed to trust no one, especially organizations and their leaders, believing that they must be self-reliant. Therefore at work, they focus on continuously gaining new skills to ensure that they remained marketable. Their goal is to have employability security, rather than job security. This mindset translates into career paths that are non-linear, involving upward, downward, and lateral moves. Unlike their boomer parents, this generation works to live rather than live to work. Gen Xers insist on balance in their lives and are generally unwilling to give a disproportionate amount of time to a job.[11] They often choose contractual, freelance, or entrepreneurial work that allows them to have a work-life balance. Also, since performance and results are a necessity for a strong resume, this cohort often looks for employment that rewards and recognizes them on performance outcomes rather than time served on the job.

In the absence of nuclear families, Gen Xers learned to fend for themselves and to create non-traditional families by bonding with friends and colleagues. Their work lives and social lives blend together to create a casual environment where the boundaries between work and play are blurred.

Gen Xers believe they will be more successful and more satisfied if they take care of themselves—a mindset that leads many in this generation to business ownership. "Twice as many young people would rather own their own business than be a top executive of a large company, and four times as many say they would rather own their own business than hold an important position in politics or government."[12] This desire to manage and control their future, coupled with a lack of trust for formal institutions, has translated into Gen Xers being one of the largest groups of financial investors in their retirement. This cohort doesn't expect or believe that the government will bankroll their retirement. Among those under thirty years old, 41 percent rate registered retirement savings plans as their number 1 source of income when they retire, compared to 26 percent among Canadians as a whole.[13] There are also other financial indicators that demonstrate this generation's focus on financial security. Rates of homeownership among this group are also greater than for Boomers at the same age. Twenty-three percent of unmarried Gen Xers owned their own homes in 1998, unlike Boomers who never hit above 21 percent.[14]

The main Gen X characteristic of independence strongly influences personal decisions as well. Even though a majority of young people indicate that they want to get married and aspire to have lasting marriages, statistics show a delay in making a formal commitment to marriage. The number of single males and females increased between 2000 and 2004.[15]

The main Gen X characteristic of independence strongly influences personal decisions as well. Even though a majority of young people indicate that they want to get married and aspire to have lasting marriages, statistics show a delay in making a formal commitment to marriage. The number of single males and females increased between 2000 and 2004.[16] Consequently, childbearing rates have also increased. The average age American women give birth for the first time is 25.1 years which has risen from 21.4 since 1970.[17] Canadian women give birth for the first time at 28 years old, which has risen from 26.9 in the last two decades. [18]

As this generation enters into its forties, we can expect to see Gen Xers influence corporate culture by expanding the application of the free-agent, job-oriented, performance-based work ethic, where results are rewarded. Gen Xers continue to integrate technology into their everyday activities as a way of juggling their personal and professional lives. Having emphasized the expectation of a balanced lifestyle, this cohort creates new, flexible, and adaptable ways to live that are based on individual choice rather than social norms. Overall, this generation places a greater demand on employers to create a workplace culture that is focused on achieving a work-life balance.

Profile of a Gen Xer

Tony is a thirty-two-year-old who just bought his first home. Up until three months ago, he lived at home with his parents. Tony finished university in the mid-90s and found that there were few jobs for new graduates. He had been told that environmental engineering would be a booming field, so he thought that he would be highly employable after graduation. Unfortunately, the recession happened so there were lots of other engineers with years of experience under their belts that he was competing with. After searching for a job for a few months, Tony decided to take a trip to Italy, where his parents emigrated from forty years ago. He traveled around the country for several weeks, visiting relatives and learning about his cultural background. Then he spent two years teaching English as a second language in Korea. During his time abroad, he met many interesting people with interesting careers, and decided that perhaps engineering might not be his calling.

Tony had always been interested in the music business, so he decided to look for work in that field. When he returned home, he found a job at a local record company as a production coordinator. Since he did not have experience or training in the music business, Tony knew he would need to prove himself and work his way up. He liked the casual, relaxed environment at work where he could interact with colleagues from across the organization, but felt that often decisions were based on office politics rather than performance. Tony's parents were disappointed that after investing so much time and money into his engineering degree, he was not applying these skills.

However, Tony was motivated by the possibilities for growth and saw his new line of work as just one-step in a long and flexible career path. After a year of hard work, Tony received a promotion and pay increase. After a few months, he felt he was ready for another challenge. He knew that he couldn't move any further within his current organization without having to pay his dues for at least a few more years, and that just seemed like too long. So, Tony updated his resume with his latest skills and results, and began to look for work. Because the economy had improved since graduation, it wasn't difficult for him to find work. He chose to move to a smaller, independent firm where he would be able to take on more responsibility and be more creative. So far, Tony is happy, but he knows that he needs to constantly prepare for his next career move since nothing is a sure thing.

ING DIRECT

ING DIRECT, an online financial services company, whose workforce is comprised mostly of Gen Xers, recognized the need to understand this generation's values, expectations, and behaviors in order to increase engagement, retention, and recruitment. Well known for their innovative employee programs designed to create a fun and engaging work environment, ING DIRECT became aware, through employee surveys and focus groups, that they needed to better address the needs of their young workforce. Managers underwent training to understand the generational differences between Gen Xers and Baby Boomers and learnt how best to collaborate with and motivate employees to ensure strong team and organizational success.

Gen Ys as the Bubble-Wrapped Youth That No One Wants to Let Go

Gen Ys		
Life-defining Events	Attitudes, Values, and Expectations	Key Characteristics
♦ Oklahoma City bombing	♦ Confidence	♦ Techno-savvy
♦ Death of Princess Diana	♦ Diversity	♦ Collective action
♦ School violence	♦ Civic duty	♦ Expressive and tolerant of differences
♦ The digital age	♦ Optimism	
♦ Corporate and government scandals	♦ Immediate access to information and services	♦ Eager to accept challenges
♦ Reality TV		♦ Innovative and creative
♦ Y2K		
♦ 9/11		
♦ U.S.-led War on Terror		

Gen Y, born between 1981and 2000 is often referred to as Nexters, Millennials, Echo Boomers, or the Net Generation. If Gen Xers were the "lost" generation, Gen Ys are the "found" generation. Two-thirds of this generation were planned for and wanted by their parents.[19] In contrast to their older siblings, this cohort is growing up in an era focused on child development, with an emphasis on building self-esteem by parents, educators, and counselors.[20]

Unlike the latchkey kids of the '70s, Gen Ys have been escorted and supervised by cautious parents who are extremely protective and involved in their children's lives. From birth, this cohort has been educated on the dangers of society. Kidnapping, school violence, and drugs have impacted their perception of safety and security. They view the world as a dangerous place. Since many parents are still at work when their children come home from school, parents fill the after school hours with activities, lessons, and programs. The term *over-scheduled child* refers to this generation. Many Gen Ys are being raised in a peer-to-peer relationship by Baby Boomer parents. Gen Ys' opinions, ideas, and suggestions are being solicited, listened to, and acted upon at home and at school. Abandoning the authoritative parenting style many Boomers experienced as children, many have opted for an open, collaborative relationship with their children. The result is an "intellectual conviction that you should not over-regulate your kids."[21]

At school, the pedagogy has shifted from a dictatorial model to an open, collaborative one where students are encouraged to give feedback to teachers and attention is paid to their interests, opinions, and ideas. To build high levels of self-esteem, today's students rarely receive negative feedback about their performance. Instead, weaknesses are positioned as positive opportunities for growth, and they have the opportunity for do-overs if they don't succeed the first time on an assignment.

Gen Ys have become accustomed to having their demands met and championed by their parents. At colleges and universities, the faculty is often shocked by parents' involvement in their children's school life. Parents request to stay on campus with their children during orientation week, and parents call the faculty to dispute grades or complete assignments on their children's behalf. In contrast to the fierce independence Gen Xers exhibit, Gen Ys are comfortable having their parents actively participate in all facets of their lives, which trickles over into the workplace.

For many Gen Ys, their primary influencers are family members, with 40 percent of teens citing a family member, usually a parent, as their role model.[22] Eighty-two percent of Gen Ys name their grandparents' generation (the Traditionalists) as the generation they trust the most. Their strong relationship with parents and grandparents allows Gen Ys to bounce ideas off them, to turn to them as mentors, and to use them as a resource by tapping into their family's endless desire to help them reach their goals. As children of increasingly interracial and multicultural relationships, this generation is more open-minded and tolerant of differences in race, religion, culture, sexual orientation, or economic status than any other generation. Gen Ys have established relationships that extend beyond social and cultural lines. Also, as the first truly global citizens, technology has empowered this generation to create and maintain close relationships through virtual communities and chat rooms with people in different neighborhoods, culture groups, and countries. Pen pal programs are no longer needed to introduce children to other cultures. Most have chat pals already. Communicating with a friend halfway around the world only requires an Internet connection.

Digital technology has fundamentally impacted this generation. Not surprisingly, the age group with the most Internet users is fifteen—to nineteen-year-olds, with 90 percent of teens reporting usage.[23] Ninety-four percent of youth (between grades 4 and 11) have access to the Internet at home. They rely on the Internet to explore social roles, stay connected with friends, and develop their social networks. By the time students reach grade 11, over 50 percent have their own Internet connection, separate from their families. Online experiences such as gaming and instant chat are seen as positive by Gen Ys. Indicating, "It made me feel good about myself," and "It makes me feel more connected to people."[24] This reinforces the fact that for Gen Ys, technology creates a sense of community and connectedness to others and fosters positive self-esteem.

Growing up in a world where they can have access to almost everything 24/7, Gen Ys are accustomed to getting what they want, when they want it. They have never known a time when they couldn't access money via an ATM or do research for a school project in the middle of the night because they can access what they need online. Technology has evolved to provide fully personalized experiences. This generation personalizes their Web pages, cell phone ring tones, the color of their iPods, and the type of information they receive and access through podcasting, personalized portals, and advertising. The Gen Y experience is an all-about-me experience. While Boomers and Gen Xers remember waiting to use the phone to call a friend, Gen Ys send an instant message to dozens of friends, talk on their cell phone, read a text message, send an e-mail, play an online game with a friend in Bangladesh, and watch TV—all at the same time. This cohort is not just technologically literate, they are techno-savvy. They have taken the skill of multitasking to a new level. Their ability to absorb information from a variety of simultaneous sources is impressive. This enables them to quickly adapt to changes in the workplace and to soak up large quantities of information.

As Gen Ys enter into the workforce, they demand a supportive environment where they are set up for success and are regularly provided with feedback. They expect an organization to solicit their opinions and ideas and to take action on them. Their goal is to find work and create a life that has meaning. This requires that employers provide a big picture context to the work that younger employees are doing. Organizational changes will be viewed by Gen Ys as positive and common place. They will create a workplace culture where diversity is not just tolerated, but celebrated.

Profile of a Gen Y

Crystal is sixteen years old and has two younger siblings. She lives with her parents in a safe, picturesque suburb. Crystal is a good student but worries that her marks will not be strong enough to get her into the university of her choice. Biology has always interested her, and she would like to one day be a marine biologist, working with whales. She has already spent a lot of time online researching what marine biologists do and where they work. Her parents have arranged that she take a trip next school break to Hawaii to participate in a month-long student program to get hands-on experience. Crystal knows that she can do anything she wants, so she wants to make sure she picks a job that will be fun and exciting. She doesn't want to work in a bank like her dad or be a real estate agent like her mom.

Crystal hasn't had time for a part-time job yet, but she would like to start to make some extra money. Between school, dance class twice a week, and violin lessons, she has little free time. Crystal and her friends, both guys and girls, often do things together as a large group—movies, bowling, parties. She is upset that next year she won't be able to see them as often since some of her friends will be moving away to go to university. But she figures that through text messaging, blogs, chat, and e-mail that they will stay best friends. She is really glad that she has her own computer and cell phone so she can always stay connected with her friends.

Crystal is nervous about leaving home; she has never been away without her parents. She is excited about the trip to Hawaii but wonders if she can take the flight by herself. Her mom has offered to go with her if she would like. Crystal and her mom get along really well. They shop together at the mall, sometimes even sharing clothes, and like to go for manicures together every couple of weeks. Once a week, the whole family goes out for dinner and a movie. When Crystal and her younger brothers fight about which movie to see, Crystal and her mom will watch the movie they like best, while her dad and the boys watch something else.

Crystal is excited about getting older, getting her own car, and being able to go out on dates, but she isn't sure she is ready to move away to school just yet. She is planning to talk about it with her grandmother this weekend. She has always received great advice from her.

Packaged Goods Manufacturer

A global packaged goods manufacturer has made a commitment to focus on the workforce of the future by understanding how generational differences impact HR practices across the employee life cycle. In addition, managers have been trained on how to leverage the skills of each generation while managing the differences. The organization has focused specifically on ensuring Gen Ys are set up for success by helping this cohort understand how to navigate the business environment through an explorative workshop. The program allows new hires to undercover how the values, expectations, and motivations of the older generations differ from their own. They learn how they can best fit within the organizational culture while making valuable contributions for change.

n-gen People Performance Inc.
Corporate Information

n-gen People Performance Inc. partners with clients to create integrated people strategies that improve metrics throughout the employee life cycle. n-gen delivers keynote presentations, workshops and designs end-to-end solutions to improve metrics and increase organizational engagement in:

- Recruitment
- Orienation
- Total rewards programs
- Employee brand promises
- Career-pathing
- Learning and development
- Mentoring
- Performance management
- Succession planning
- Management practices

If you would like more information on n-gen People Performance Inc.'s products and services, please visit our website at *www.ngenperformance.com* or contact us Toll Free at 1-877-362-7564

Sign up on our website to participate in community of practice blogs based on each section discussed in *Loyalty Unplugged*.

Notes

Introduction

1   Society for Human Resource Management. "Closing the Gap," *Fortune* November 15, 2005.

Chapter 1

1   Thomas Davenport, *Human Capital* (San Francisco: Jossey-Bassey, 1999), chap. 2.

2   Peter Capelli, *The New Employment Deal: Managing the Market Driven Workforce* (Boston: Harvard Business School Press, 1999).

3   Ibid., 116.

4   Ibid., 21.

5   "Lots of It About—Corporate Social Responsibility," Special report, *The Economist* vol. 365, issue 8303 (December 14, 2002): 74.

6   Ed Michaels et al., *The War for Talent* (Boston: Harvard Business School Press, 2001).

7   Capelli, *The New Employment Deal*, chap. 1, 17-48.

8   William B. R. Robson, *Aging Populations and the Workforce: Challenges for Employers* (Manitoba: British-North America Committee, 2001).

9   Conference Board of Canada, *Performance and Potential 2001-2002: Charting a Canadian Course in North America* (Ottawa, CA, 2001), 55.

10   Arlene Dohm, "Gauging the Labor Force Effects of Retiring Baby-Boomers," *Monthly Labor Review*, July 2000, 25.

11   Daniel Eisenberg, "The Coming Job Boom: The Help Wanted Ads May Look Thin—But Thanks to Aging Baby Boomers, That's about to Change," *Time*, May 6, 2002, 40.

[12]   Dohm, "Gauging the Labor Force," 17-25

[13]   Human Resources Development Canada. *Challenges of an Aging Workforce: An Overview of the Issue* (PowerPoint presentation, Canada, May 2002).

[14]   Raizil Robin and John Gray, "Tomorrow's Hot Jobs," *Canadian Business* vol. 77, issue 5 (March 1-14, 2004): 37.

[15]   Dohm, "Gauging the labor force," 17.

[16]   Eisenberg, "The Coming Job Boom."

[17]   Conference Board of Canada, *Performance and Potential*, 59.

[18]   Conference Board of Canada, *Performance and Potential*, 51.

[19]   Frank Horwitz, "Finders, Keepers? Attracting, Motivating, and Retaining Knowledge Workers," *Human Resource Management* vol.13, no.4 (2003).

[20]   Timothy A. Judge and Lise M. Saari, "Employee Attitudes and Job Satisfaction," *Human Resource Management* vol. 43, no. 4 (2004): 295-407.

        Interestingly, numerous studies have shown there is a correlation between job description and employees leaving an organization.

[21]   Global consulting houses such as Watson Wyatt, Towers Perrin, Hewitt, and the Gallup Group.

[22]   This is even truer of those that belong to the Gen X and Gen Y who hold little affinity to the actual organization; rather, they are loyal to their managers and colleagues.

[23]   These qualities are not a suggested replacement to existing organization values or competencies. The three characteristics of transparency, responsiveness, and partnering can be layered onto existing organizational competencies and values. They are a measuring stick with which your organization can assess your success of executing your corporate values or competencies. For example, if one of your organizational values is integrity, then how is your organization demonstrating transparency, responsiveness, and partnering when acting with integrity. To assess this, a question a manager can ask is, When demonstrating integrity, am I being transparent, responsive, and partnering with my team? For a more detailed discussion between values and the engagement characteristics, please read the chapter on employee brand promises.

Chapter 2

[1] What is critical to remember in defining a generation is that even though some events impact almost every group in society irrespective of age (like the attacks of September 11, 2001), these events tend to have the strongest impact on young adults. They are the life-defining events for those coming of age during that time.

[2] Chester, E. *Employing Generation Why?*. (Colorado: Tucker House Books, 2002, p.12)

[3] U.S. Bureau of the Census, *2000 Population by Age and by Gender*, 2000 Census Summary File 1 (Washington DC, 2000).

[4] The remaining population percentage represents those under six years old and eighty-five years and above.

[5] Statistics Canada, "Population by sex and age group," CANSIM table 051-0001, 2005.

[6] The remaining population percentage represents those under six years old and eighty-five years and above.

[7] Compas Inc., "The Loyalty of Young Employees: How Low and Why?" *Financial Post*, Winter 2003, 3.

[8] Ibid., 2.

[9] Ellen Lorian Kratz, "The Gray Flannel Office: Fifty Years Ago Happiness Was a Job at a Very Big Company—a look back at the days when the FORTUNE 500 was young and the Organization Man reigned supreme," *Fortune* vol. 150, issue 12 (December 13, 2004): 152.

Section II: How to Get 'Em

[1] Long W. Lam and Louis P. White, "Human Resource Orientation and Corporate Performance," *Human Resource Development Quarterly* vol. 9, no. 4 (Winter 1998).

[2] Derek Chapman, "Recruiting in Tight Labour Markets," *HR Professional*, April-May 2006.

[3] Drake Beam Morin Inc., *Holding on to High Performers: A Strategic Approach to Retention* (New York: Drake Beam Morin Inc., 2000).

[4] Sandy French, "Oriented or Disoriented?" *Canadian HR Reporter* vol. 14, no. 22 (December 17, 2001): 6.

Chapter 3

[1]   Daniel W. Greening and Daniel B. Turnban, "Corporate Social Performance as a Competitive Advantage in Attracting a Quality Workforce," *Business and Society* vol. 39, no. 3 (September 2000).

[2]   Jeff Taylor, "A Monster Success," *The Economist* vol. 370 (March 27, 2004): 66.

[3]   "RD2 Helps Southwest Airlines Launch First Airline Weblog," Southwest Airlines news release, May 24, 2006. http://www.southwest.com/about_swa/press/prindex.html.

[4]   Ann Marie Ryan and Nancy T. Tippings, "Attracting and Selecting: What Psychological Research Tells Us," *Human Resource Management* vol. 43, no. 4 (Winter 2004): 305-318.

[5]   Coleman H. Peterson. "Employee Retention: The Secrets Behind Wal-Mart's Successful Hiring Policies," *Human Resource Management* vol. 44, no. 1 (Spring 2005): 85-88.

[6]   Ryan and Tippings, "Attracting and Selecting," 305-318.

[7]   Derek Chapman, "Recruiting in Tight Labour Markets," *HR Professional*, April-May 2006.

[8]   Drake Beam Morin Inc. *Holding on to High Performers: A Strategic Approach to Retention* (New York: Drake Beam Morin Inc., 2000).

[9]   Pfizer Web site, http://www.pfizer.com/pfizer/are/careers/mn_working_vision.jsp.

[10] Peterson, "Employee Retention," 85-88.

[11] Daniel M. Cable, Lynda Aiman-Smith, Paul W. Mulvey, and Jeffrey R. Edwards, "The Sources and Accuracy of Job Applicants' Beliefs about Organizational Culture," *Academy of Management Journal* vol. 43, no. 6 (December 2000).

[12] Ontario Power Generation Web site, http://www.mypowercareer.com.

[13] Daniel M. Cable and Daniel B. Turnban, "The Value of Organizational Reputation in the Recruitment Context: A Brand-Equity Perspective," *Journal of Applied Social Psychology* vol. 33, no. 11 (2003): 2260.

[14] Shell Canada Web site, "How we Work," http://www.shell.ca/home.

[15] Ryan and Tippings, "Attracting and Selecting."

[16] Mike Martin, "Friend in Need? Potential Colleague Indeed," *Globe and Mail*, April 21, 2005.

[17] Ryan and Tippings, "Attracting and Selecting."

[18] Elizabeth Lincoln, *Maximizing your R.O.E: Summit on The Mature Workforce Executing the Strategy* (Cendant Car Rental Group presentation at the Summit on the Mature Workforce Conference, Toronto, Ontario, Canada, September 19, 2005).

Chapter 4

[1] Sue Nador, "Successful Onboarding—From 'I Do' to 'Happily Ever After,'" *HR Professional*, August-September 2006.

[2] Coleman H. Peterson, "Employee Retention: The Secrets behind Wal-Mart's Successful Hiring Policies," *Human Resource Management* vol. 44, no. 1 (Spring 2005): 87.

Chapter 5

[1] Leigh Branham, *7 Hidden Reasons Employees Leave: How to Recognize the Subtle Signs and Act before Its Too Late* (New York: AMACOM, 2005) and Phani Tej Adidam, "Causes and Consequences of High Turnover by Sales Professionals," *Journal of American Academy of Business* vol. 10, issue 1(September 2006): 137-141.

[2] Michael N. Abrams, "Employee Retention Strategies: Lessons from the Best," *Healthcare Executive* vol. 19, issue 4 (July-August 2004): 18.

[3] Mercer Management Consulting, *European Total Rewards Survey*, September 2005.

[4] Chartered Institute of Personnel and Development (CIPD) Web site. http://www.cipd.co.uk/subjects/pay/general/totrewdqf.htm.

[5] Abrams, "Employee Retention Strategies," 18.

Chapter 6

[1] Conference Board Inc., *Engaging Employees Through Your Brand* (New York: Conference Board Inc., 2001), 13.

[2] Sandy French, "No HR Strategy Is Complete without Brand Alignment," *Canadian HR Reporter* vol. 14, issue 19 (November 5, 2003): 13.

[3] Conference Board, *Engaging Employees*, 10.

[4] Patricia K. Zingheim and Jay R. Schuster, "Creating a Powerful Customized Workplace Reward Brand," *Compensation and Benefits Review* vol. 33, issue 6 (November-December 2001): 30.

5   Harvest Consulting Group, *BrandSense™: Building Brands with Sensory Experience* (New York: Harvest Consulting Group, 2001).

6   Alan Drake, "Building Connected Organizations: A Key Element in Improving Workplace Performance in the Context of the Business," *Journal of Corporate Real Estate* vol. 5, issue 2 (April 2003): 107.

7   Harvest Consulting Group, *BrandSense™*.

8   "HR Brand Building in Today's Market," Cover story, *HR Focus* vol. 82, issue 2 (February 2005): 1.

9   French, "No HR Strategy," 13.

10   Conference Board, *Engaging Employees*, 33.

11   An important cautionary note is that most lists are created or adjudicated by large HR consulting houses. While they may work in conjunction with a business or trade magazine or newspaper, the work of evaluating the organization is done by consulting houses. For the skeptical Gen Xer authors, there appears to be a conflict of interest. With some lists, we have noted that either many of the organizations on the list are already clients of the particular HR house. Or in interacting with organization leaders, we learn that the consulting house, upon learning about areas of opportunity, obviously focus on business development. While the average employee may not make the connection of the potential conflict of interest, your organization should be aware that socially responsible Gen Ys may not approve.

12   Zingheim and Schuster, "Creating a Powerful," 30.

13   Conference Board of Canada, *Performance and Potential 2001-2002: Charting a Canadian Course in North America* (Ottawa, CA, 2001), 20.

14   Conference Board, *Engaging Employees*, 15.

15   Bill Faust and Beverly Bethge. "Looking Inward: How Internal Branding and Communications Affect Cultural Change," *Design Management Journal* vol. 14, issue 3 (Summer 2003).

16   French, "No HR Strategy," 13.

Section IV: How to Grow 'Em

[1] Frank D. Fredric, Richard P. Finnegan, and Craig R. Tyalor. "The Race for Talent: Retaining and Engaging Workers in the Twenty-first Century," *Human Resource Planning* vol. 27, no. 3 (2004): 13.

[2] Towers Perrin, *Look Closer: Managing Today's Talent to Create Tomorrow's Leaders* (New York:Towers Perrin, 2004), 2.

[3] A debate exists on how, what, and when to communicate to someone that they are considered top talent. While your organization may not clearly label high-potential (see chapter on succession planning), a talent management strategy should allow for manager- and self-identification of knowledge, skills, and experience.

[4] Towers Perrin, *Look Closer*, 4.

[5] Stephen Heinen and Colleen O'Neill, "Managing Talent to Maximize Performance," *Employment Relations Today*, Summer 2004, 68.

Chapter 7

[1] Claudine Kapel and Catherine Shepherd, "Career Ladders Create Common Language for Defining Jobs," *Canadian HR Reporter* vol. 17, no. 12 (June 14, 2004): 15-16.

[2] Ibid.

[3] Marc Iskowitz, "Raised Well in Pharam," *Medical Marketing and Media* vol. 41, issue 9 (September 2006): 84-86.

[4] Arieh Bonder, "Competency-Based Management in Service Canada" (presentation at Infonex Conference, Ottawa, Ontario, Canada, May 18, 2006).

[5] Robert Morison, Tamara Erickson, and Ken Dychtwald, "Managing Middlescence," *Harvard Business Review*, March 2006, 80.

Chapter 8

[1] Kristine Ellis, "Individual Development Plans: The Building Blocks of Development," *Training*, December 2004, 22,and 24.

[2] Kurt Kraiger, Daniel McLinden, and Wendy J. Casper, "Collaborative Planning for Training Impact," *Human Resource Management* vol. 43, no. 4 (Winter 2004): 341.

3   Robert Fulmer and Jay A. Conger. "Developing Leaders with 2020 Vision: Companies Can Develop Deep, Enduring Bench Strength by Combining Succession Planning and Leadership Development to Create a Long-term Process for Managing the Talent Roster," *Financial Executive* vol. 20, issue 5 (July-August 2004): 40.

4   Fredric D. Frank and Craig R. Taylor. "Talent Management: Trends That Will Shape the Future," *Human Resource Planning* vol. 27, no. 1 (2004): 33-41.

5   Craig King, "Intrapreneurship: Heady Business," Sun Developer Network Web site, January 28, 2004. http://developers.sun.com/toolkits/articles/intrapreneur.html.

6   Virginia Galt, "Harness Talents of Middle Managers," *The Globe and Mail*, March 25, 2005.

Chapter 9

1   Therese A. Joiner, Timothy Bartman, and Terese Garreffa. "The Effects of Mentoring on Perceived Career Success, Commitment, and Turnover Intentions," *The Journal of American Academy of Business*, September 2004, 164-170.

2   Howard Wolosky, "Mentoring the Formal Approach Payoff," *Practical Accountant*, January 2005, 32.

3   Ibid., 29-32.

4   Ibid., 32.

5   Kym Wolfe, "Mentor Magic," *HR Professional*, June-July 2005, 28.

Chapter 10

1   Julie Jasica-Mercola, Brian J. McIntyre, and Julie M. Womack, "Maximizing Business Results through Performance Management." Published by Towers Perrin in association with PeopleSoft, January 2003, 1.

2   Richard Greenberg and Luellen Lucid, "Beyond Performance Management: Four Principles of Performance Leadership," *Workspan* vol. 47, no. 9 (September 2004): 43.

3   Towers Perrin, *Perspectives on People: Performance and Rewards* (New York: Towers Perrin, 2002).

4   Greenberg and Lucid, "Beyond Performance Management," 43.

5   Liane Davey, Nancy Gore, and Owen Parker, "Reaching Productive Engagement: The Four\ Pillar Approach to Managing Investment in Human Capital," *Ivey Business Journal*, July-August 2003, 1-5.

6   Ibid.

Chapter 11

[1] Dianne Jacobs, "In Search of Future Leaders: Managing the Global Talent Pipeline," *Ivey Business Journal Online*, March-April 2005, 1. Dianne Jacobs is principal, Human Resources, Goldman Sachs JBWere, Melbourne, Australia.

[2] Carson F. Dye, "Is Anyone Next in Line? Succession Plans Are Critical to Ensuring a Smooth Transition When an Organization Faces an Unexpected—or an Expected—Leadership Vacancy," *Healthcare Financial Management* vol. 59, no. 12 (February 2005): 64. Carson F. Dye is senior vice president and central region codirector of Witt/Kiefer, Toledo, Ohio. While this article focuses mainly on succession-planning senior executives, the principles can be driven further down in the organization.

[3] Thomas Hoffman, "Grooming the Next Generation: Smart IT Leaders Take Succession Planning Seriously," *Computerworld* vol. 39, issue 21 (May 23, 2005): 39.

[4] Ibid.

[5] Institute of Management and Administration, "A Succession Planning Model That Can Work for You (Case Study)," *HR Focus* vol. 881, issue 3 (March 2004): 5.

[6] Michelle Salob, Shelli Greenslade, and Marc Effron, *Research Highlights: How the Top 20 Companies Grow Great Leaders* (N.p.: Hewitt Associates, 2005). According to Hewitt's report, "How the Top 20 Companies Grow Great Leaders," other organizations that focus on leadership development include 3M, Johnson & Johnson, Dell Inc., Liz Clairborne Inc., American Express Company, Pitney Bowes Inc., and Pfizer Inc., among others.

[7] Michelle Salob, Shelli Greenslad, and Marc Effron, *Research Highlights: How the Top 20 Companies Grow Great Leaders* (N.p.: Hewitt Associates, 2005). The high TSR are those companies whose measure is in the seventy-fifth percentile and above. The companies with a low score fell into the twenty-fifth percentile and below.

[8] Institute of Management and Administration, "A Succession Planning Model."

[9] Hoffman, "Grooming the Next Generation," 39.

[10] International City-County Management Association, "If I Pass the Baton, Who Will Grab It? Creating Bench Strength in Public Management," *Public Management* vol. 87, issue 8 (September 2005): 8.

11   It is best to have assessment mechanisms that are both self and management driven. Assessments would include, but are not limited to, performance management, 360-degree feedback, personality tests, and individual interviews.

Chapter 12

1   Marcus Buckingham and Curt Coffman, *First, Break All the Rules: What the World's Greatest Managers Do Differently* (New York: Simon & Schuster, 1999).

2   Frank M. Horwitz, Chan Teng Heng, and Hesan Ahmed Quazi. "Finders, Keepers? Attracting, Motivating, and Retaining Knowledge Workers," *Human Resource Management Journal* vol. 13, no. 4 (2003): 28.

3   J. R. Katzenbach and D. K. Smith, *The Wisdom of Teams: Creating the High-Performance Organization* (Boston: Harvard Business School, 1993).

4   Coaching is not about helping a direct report to overcome personal or emotional challenges, a process to change the employee without their involvement, teaching a new skill (this is achieved through learning and development), or a tool for performance management.

Appendix

1   William H. Whyte, *The Organization Man* (New York: Doubleday, 1956).

2   Ellen Florian Kratz, "The Gray Flannel Office: Fifty Years Ago Happiness Was a Job at a Very Big Company," *Fortune* vol. 150, issue 12 (December 13, 2004): 152.

3   Virginia Galt, "Home Depot to Build on Base of Mature Workers," *The Globe and Mail*, February 16, 2005.

4   Baby boomers are often divided into two cohorts, which include the first half and the second half boomers. The division is used to distinguish between those born in the '40s and early '50s who actively participated in the events of the '60s and those born in the mid-'50s and early '60s who were too late to participate in Woodstock and other movements. For our purposes, we reference this generation as one cohort; however, recognize that there are distinctions between younger and older boomers.

5   Rod Zemke, Claire Raines, and Bob Filipczak. *Generations at Work: Managing the Clash of Veterans, Boomers, Xers and Nexters in Your Workplace* (New York: McGraw-Hill, 2000).

6   This too can be a factor why some experts want to divide the baby boomers into two cohorts, as the younger half would have experienced some of the corporate reforms during their coming-of-age period.

7   Neil Howe and William Strauss, *"The New Generation Gap,"Atlantic Monthly*, December 1997, 67-68.

8   Statistics Canada, "Family Structure, by provinces and territories (1991 and 1996 Censuses)," 2004.

9   Robert M. Orrange, "Individualism, Family Values, and the Professional Middle Class: In-depth Interviews with Advanced Law and MBA Students," *The Sociology Quarterly* vol. 4, no. 3 (2003): 451-480.

10   Stephen Craig and Stephen Earl Benette, *After the Boom: The Politics of Generation X* (London: Rowman & Littlefield Publishers Inc., 1997).

11   Zemke, Raines, and Filipczak, *Generations at Work*.

12   Richard Miniter, "Generation X Does Business," *The American Enterprise for Public Policy Research* vol. 8, no. 4 (July-August 1997): 38.

13   Compas Inc., "Pension and Retirement Study," *National Post* poll, February 2004.

14   Alison S. Wellnes, "Gen X Homes In," *American Demographics*, August 1999, 57-62.

15   Statistics Canada, "Population by marital status and sex," CANSIM table 051-0010, 2005.

16   Statistics Canada, "Population by marital status and sex," CANSIM table 051-0010, 2005.

17   National Vital Statistics Reports, "Births: Final Data for 2002" U.S. Department of Health and Human Services vol. 52, no.10 (December 2003): 2

18   Statistics Canada, "Births," *The Daily*, July 12, 2005.

19   Zemke, Raines, and Filipczak, *Generations at Work*, 130.

20   Carolyn Martin and Bruce Tulgan, *Managing the Generation Mix* (Amherst, MA: HRD Press, 2002).

21   Michelle Quinn, "Are We Raising a Generation of Spoiled, Out of Control Children," *Knight Ridder Newspaper*, February 3, 2004, 1. http://www.azcentral.com.

22   Kaja Perina, "Where Have All the Idols Gone?" *Psychology Today* vol. 37, issue 4 (August 2004): 3.

23   Heather Dryburgh, "Changing Our Ways: Why and How Canadians Use the Internet," Statistics Canada, catalogue no. 56F0006XIE.

24   Erin Research Inc., "Young Canadians in a Wired World, Phase II Student Survey," Media Awareness Network, November 2005, 39.

Bibliography

Bonder, Arieh. "Competency-Based Management in Service Canada." Presentation at Infonex Conference, Ottawa, Ontario, Canada, May 18, 2006.

Buckingham, Marcus, and Curt Coffman. *First, Break All the Rules: What the World's Greatest Managers Do Differently.* New York: Simon & Schuster, 1999.

Cable, Daniel M., Lynda Aiman-Smith, Paul W. Mulvey, and Jeffrey R. Edwards. "The Sources and Accuracy of Job Applicants' Beliefs about Organizational Culture, Academy of Management," *Journal of Applied Psychology* vol. 43, no. 6 (December 2000).

Cable, Daniel M., and Daniel B. Turnban. "The Value of Organizational Reputation in the Recruitment Context: A Brand-Equity Perspective," *Journal of Applied Social Psychology* vol. 33, no.11 (2003).

Chapman, Derek. "Recruiting in Tight Labour Markets," *HR Professional,* April-May 2006.

Chester, E. *Employing Generation Why?.* (Colorado: Tucker House Books, 2002, p.12)

Compas Inc. "Pension and Retirement Study," *National Post* poll, February 2004.

_____. "The Loyalty of Young Employees: How Low and Why?" *Financial Post* (Winter 2003).

Craig, Stephen, and Stephen Earl Benette. *After the Boom: The Politics of Generation X.* London: Rowman & Littlefield Publishers Inc., 1997.

Davey, Liane, Nancy Gore, and Owen Parker. "Reaching Productive Engagement: The Four Pillar Approach to Managing Investment in Human Capital," *Ivey Business Journal,* July-August 2003.

Drake Beam Morin. *Holding on to High Performers: A Strategic Approach to Retention.* New York: Drake Beam Morin Inc., 2000.

Dryburgh, Heather. *Changing Our Ways: Why and How Canadians Use the Internet.* Statistics Canada, catalogue no. 56F0006XIE.

Ellis, Kristine. "Individual Development Plans: The Building Blocks of Development," *Training,* December 2004.

Fredric, Frank D., Richard P. Finnegan, and Craig R. Taylor. "The Race for Talent: Retaining and Engaging Workers in the Twenty-first Century," *Human Resource Planning* vol. 27, no. 3 (2004).

Frank, Fredric D., and Craig R. Taylor. "Talent Management: Trends That Will Shape the Future," *Human Resource Planning* vol. 27, no. 1 (2004).

French, Sandy. "Oriented or Disoriented?" *Canadian HR Reporter* vol. 14, no. 22 (December 17, 2001).

Fulmer, Robert, and Jay A. Conger. "Developing Leaders with 2020 Vision: Companies Can Develop Deep, Enduring Bench Strength by Combining Succession Planning and Leadership Development to Create a Long-term Process for Managing the Talent Roster," *Financial Executive* vol. 20, issue 5 (July-August 2004).

Galt, Virginia. "Harness Talents of Middle Managers," *Globe and Mail,* March 25, 2005.

_____. "Home Depot to Build on Base of Mature Workers," *Globe and Mail,* February 16, 2005.

Greenberg, Richard, and Luellen Lucid. "Beyond Performance Management: Four Principles of Performance Leadership," *Workspan* vol. 47, no. 9 (September 2004).

Greening, Daniel W., and Daniel B. Turnban. "Corporate Social Performance as a Competitive Advantage in Attracting a Quality Workforce," *Business and Society* vol. 39, no. 3 (September 2000).

Heinen, Stephen, and Colleen O'Neill. "Managing Talent to Maximize Performance," *Employment Relations Today*, Summer 2004.

Horwitz, Frank M., Chan Teng Heng, and Hesan Ahmed Quazi. "Finders, Keepers? Attracting, Motivating, and Retaining Knowledge Workers," *Human Resource Management Journal* vol. 13, no. 4 (2003).

Howe, Neil, and William Strauss. "The New Generation Gap," *Atlantic Monthly*, December 1997.

Iskowitz, Marc. "Raised Well in Pharam," *Medical Marketing and Media* vol. 41, issue 9 (September 2006).

Jasica-Mercola, Julie, Brian J. McIntyre, and Julie M. Womack. Maximizing Business Results through Performance Management." Published by Towers Perrin in association with PeopleSoft, January 2003.

Joiner, Therese A., Timothy Bartman, and Terese Garreffa. "The Effects of Mentoring on Perceived Career Success, Commitment, and Turnover Intentions," *The Journal of American Academy of Business* (September 2004).

Kapel, Claudine, and Catherine Shepherd. "Career Ladders Create Common Language for Defining Jobs," *Canadian HR Reporter* vol. 17, no. 12 (June 14, 2004).

Katzenbach, J. R., and D. K. Smith. *The Wisdom of Teams: Creating the High-Performance Organization.* Boston: Harvard Business School, 1993.

King, Craig. "Intrapreneurship: Heady Business," Sun Developer Network Web site, January 28, 2004. http://developers.sun.com/toolkits/articles/intrapreneur.html.

Kraiger, Kurt, Daniel McLinden, and Wendy J. Casper. "Collaborative Planning for Training Impact," *Human Resource Management* vol. 43, no. 4 (Winter 2004).

Kratz, Ellen Lorian. "The Gray Flannel Office: Fifty Years Ago Happiness Was a Job at a Very Big Company—a look back at the days when the FORTUNE 500 was young and the Organization Man reigned supreme," *Fortune* vol. 150, issue 12 (December 13, 2004).

Lam, Long W., and Louis P. White. "Human Resource Orientation and Corporate Performance," *Human Resource Development Quarterly* vol. 9, no. 4 (Winter 1998).

Lincoln, Elizabeth. "Maximizing your R.O.E: Summit on the Mature Workforce Executing the Strategy." Cendant Car Rental Group presentation at the Summit on the Mature Workforce Conference, Toronto, Ontario, Canada, September 19, 2005.

Martin, Joyce A. et al. "Births: Final Data for 2002" *National Vital Statistics Reports,* U.S. Department of Health and Human Services vol. 52, no.10 (December 2003)

Martin, Mike. "Friend in Need? Potential Colleague Indeed," *Globe and Mail,* April 21, 2005.

Miniter, Richard. "Generation X Does Business," *American Enterprise for Public Policy Research* vol. 8, no. 4 (July-August 1997).

Morison, Robert, Tamara Erickson, and Ken Dychtwald. "Managing Middlescence," *Harvard Business Review,* March 2006.

Nador, Sue. "Successful Onboarding—From 'I Do' to 'Happily Ever After'," *HR Professional,* August-September 2006.

Ontario Power Generation Web site, http://www.mypowercareer.com.

Orrange, Robert M. "Individualism, Family Values and the Professional Middle Class: In-depth Interviews with Advanced Law and MBA Students," *The Sociology Quarterly* vol. 4, num. 3 (2003).

Paul, Pamela. "Meet the Parents," *American Demographics*, January 2002.

Perina, Kaja. "Where Have All the Idols Gone?" *Psychology Today* vol. 37 (August 2004).

Peterson, Coleman H. "Employee Retention: The Secrets behind Wal-Mart's Successful Hiring Policies," *Human Resource Management* vol. 44, no.1 (Spring 2005).

Pfizer Web site, http://www.pfizer.com/pfizer/are/careers/mn_working_vision.jsp.

"RD2 Helps Southwest Airlines Launch First Airline Weblog," Southwest Airlines news release, May 24, 2006. http://www.southwest.com/about_swa/press/prindex.html.

Ryan, Ann Marie, and Nancy T. Tippings. "Attracting and Selecting: What Psychological Research Tells Us," *Human Resource Management* vol. 43, no. 4 (Winter 2004).

Shell Canada Web site, "How We Work," http://www.shell.ca/home.

Society for Human Resource Management. "Closing the Gap," *Fortune* November 15, 2005.

Statistics Canada, "Births," *The Daily*, July 12, 2005.

_____. "Family Structure, by provinces and territories (1991 and1996 Censuses)," 2004.

_____. "Population by marital status and sex," CANSIM table 051-0010, 2005.

_____. "Population by sex and age group," CANSIM table 051-0001, 2005.

_____. "Pregnancy outcomes by age group," 2005.

Taylor, Jeff. "A Monster Success," *The Economist* vol. 370 (March 27, 2004).

Towers Perrin. *Look Closer: Managing Today's Talent to Create Tomorrow's Leaders.* New York: Towers Perrin, 2004.

————. *Perspectives on People: Performance and Rewards.* New York: Towers Perrin, 2002.

U.S. Bureau of the Census. *2000 Population by Age and Gender*, 2000 Census Summary File 1 (SF1). Washington DC, 2000.

Wellner, Alison S. "Gen X Homes In," *American Demographics*, August 1999.

Whyte, William H. *The Organization Man.* New York: Doubleday, 1956.

Wolfe, Kym. "Mentor Magic," *HR Professional*, June-July 2005.

Wolosky, Howard. "Mentoring the Formal Approach Payoff," *Practical Accountant*, January 2005.

Zemke, Rod, Claire Raines, and Bob Filipczak. *Generations at Work: Managing the Clash of Veterans, Boomers, Xers, and Nexters in Your Workplace.* New York: McGraw-Hill, 2000.

Printed in the United States
81200LV00007B/19-54